Vedantic Meditation

Also by David Frawley:

Yoga and Ayurveda: Self-Healing and Self-Realization

Ayurveda and the Mind: The Healing of Consciousness

In Search of the Cradle of Civilization
(with Georg Feuerstein and Subhash Kak)

Tantric Yoga and the Wisdom Goddesses

Ayurvedic Healing: A Comprehensive Guide

The Yoga of Herbs (with Vasant Lad)

Vedantic Meditation

LIGHTING
THE FLAME
OF AWARENESS

DAVID FRAWLEY

NORTH ATLANTIC BOOKS
BERKELEY, CALIFORNIA

Vedantic Meditation

Published by
North Atlantic Books
P.O. Box 12327
Berkeley, California 94712

Cover art © Hari Dev. This type of image is known as yantra art and is used as a meditation device.
Cover and book design © Ayelet Maida, A/M Studios.
Printed in the United States of America.

Vedantic Meditation is sponsored by the Society for the Study of Native Arts and Sciences, a nonprofit educational corporation whose goals are to develop an educational and crosscultural perspective linking various scientific, social, and artistic fields; to nurture a holistic view of arts, sciences, humanities, and healing; and to publish and distribute literature on the relationship of mind, body, and nature.

Library of Congress Cataloging-in-Publication Data

Frawley, David.
  Vedantic meditation : lighting the flame of awareness / by David Frawley.
     p.   cm.
  ISBN 1-55643-334-4
  1. Meditation—Hinduism.   2. Vedanta.   I. Title

BL1238.34.F73 2000
294.5'435—dc21   00-020634

1   2   3   4   5   6   7   8   9   /   04   03   02   01   00

Contents

Foreword

I n India David Frawley is recognized as a Vedacharya, a
teacher of the Vedas. He may be the only Westerner to be
given such a title. The author of more than twenty books, Dr.
Frawley has left me in awe once again. This book imparts the
kind of authentic experience that listening to the voice of a
master does. In the West, I have for years looked to Dr. Frawley as the authority in the field of Vedic education.

In *Vedantic Meditation,* Dr. Frawley clarifies that Vedanta and
all its branches revolve around one premise: to become Self-realized through the practice of Self-inquiry. Without this understanding the practices of Yoga, Ayurveda and Jyotish are
incomplete.

We have all experienced the stillness of a mountaintop, a
valley, or a forest. At times this silence or stillness is so perva-
sive that it fills our bodies and souls with wonder. We seek
refuge in the fresh mountain air, relish the stunning views, and
cherish our precious wildlife, but it is what we feel in the wilder-
ness that attracts and rejuvenates us. The silence in the stillness
of nature is inherent in every human being.

Unfortunately stress, our fast-paced life, and our attraction to
external rather than internal reality drowns out silence from the
hearts, minds, and cell of our bodies. Frawley describes how the
spiritual journey begins by replacing your stress with silence. It
finishes with a glimpse of what can become your highest potential, leaving you with a vision of your true nature.

A hurricane, an atom, or a solar system each require a still
center to be effective. The bigger the silent center of the eye of
a hurricane, the more powerful are its winds. This silence is the

key to unlocking our full human potential as human beings. When this silence is combined with dynamic action, our potential is achieved. This is called the co-existence of opposite forces.

Scientists agree that we achieve only ten percent of our human potential. When we establish silence at the core of our activities, our potential is unlimited. In the field of athletics, when athletes perform at their ultimate best, the experience is always effortless—still, silent, in slow motion, and euphoric, coexisting with a superhuman level of activity.

For thousands of years religions around the world have taught various techniques to help us re-establish this silence at the core of our being. Religious disciplines and codes of conduct have supported these techniques and prepared the way for the direct experience of our own silence and spirituality. This understanding is most intact today in the Vedic texts and through the study of Vedanta. In Vedanta, silence is understood as our own human consciousness—which resides in our hearts and pervades everything in the universe.

According to the Vedas, the human heart, not the mind, is the seat of thought, actions, and desires. If the heart is the eye of the hurricane, the source of silence and consciousness, then the mind is like the winds of the hurricane, always restless and thinking. For most of us our mind determines what we think, how we act, and what we say. We are separated from the source of our consciousness, power, and creativity, which resides in our heart. Because we don't have our heart integrated with our thoughts, our mind and senses relentlessly seek satisfaction through the external experience.

According to the Vedas, this disconnection of mind and heart leads to all the suffering that we see in the world today. Scientists blame stress for eighty percent of our diseases, but it is our lack of silence that allows stress to be so dominant in our lives. This is why, Dr. Frawley points out, having a meditation practice in your life is so important.

The health benefits of meditation are enough of an incentive to start a practice. But even more compelling is the change in the quality of life when you start to experience the hurricane effect of meditation. Soon, doing less and accomplishing more becomes a way of life, and the wrath of stress rolls off your body like water off a duck's back. With stress under control, you may be inclined toward further Self-inquiry. This is the beginning of your spiritual journey.

David Frawley's gift is to be able to describe the source, course, and goal of spirituality. The source of our spirituality is our own consciousness. The goal is to experience it in your self, to realize your true nature and access your full potential. The course material to achieve this state is the technique of Vedantic Meditation.

Vedantic Meditation is required reading for anyone on a spiritual path. It is a pure and authentic depiction of Vedanta, the essence of the most ancient scriptures in the world, the Vedas.

John Douillard
Director of Player Development,
New Jersey Nets
June, 2000

Preface

Meditation is an important practice in spirituality and healing throughout the world today. The central role of India in many of the world's meditation traditions is well known, as this region is the origin of various Hindu, Buddhist, Jain and Sikh meditation traditions. However, Vedanta, India's oldest meditation tradition, is not always understood or given its proper place, though it was probably the first Eastern meditation tradition to come to the West, arriving more than a century ago through Swami Vivekananda.

The purpose of the present book is to introduce or reintroduce Vedanta in a personal and experiential manner so that the reader can come to a living and direct connection with the teaching. It is not an academic presentation examining the subject from a conceptual or historical angle. Nor is it a traditional presentation elucidating technical terms in a systematic manner for specially trained and prepared students.

Many of us in the West today find it difficult to penetrate Indian texts and their precise but dense terminology, all of which reflects a very different cultural background. Nor can we understand the older languages like Sanskrit in which these views are best explained. Yet many of us do have the intelligence to grasp their insights if they are given in a contemporary language in a style relative to the psychological issues of our daily lives.

This book emphasizes the practical side of Vedanta as a way of meditation, which is the real essence of the teaching. Its explication of meditation is fluid, showing a many-sided view of Vedanta and the philosophy's complete understanding of human nature. The Vedantic way of meditative inquiry unfolds through

...nd contemplations. The book is divided into four secti...

1. The first secti... examines the background of Vedanta and its main method of Self-inquiry.

2. The second section deals with specific topics, usually one or two pages in length, concerning prime issues and concerns of the contemporary spiritual path.

3. The third section contains short discussions about issues and methods of meditation practice.

4. The fourth section presents the teachings of Ramana Maharshi, perhaps the best known and respected modern Vedantic teacher and the most famous Self-realized sage of modern India.

May this small volume serve to link us with sages, who ever remain within our deeper consciousness as the flame that gives meaning to our life, love and striving!

David Frawley (Vamadeva Shastri)
Santa Fe, New Mexico
January 2000

PART I

Vedantic Meditation

From darkness lead us to light, from non-being
lead us to being, from death lead us to
immortality.

Brihadaranyaka Upanishad I.3.28

I laud the flame of awareness that is placed
before all things, the deity of the sacred ritual,
who manifests by the seasons, the invoker of the
Gods, best to grant the treasure.

The flame is the invoker, the seer-will, the
manifold knowledge of truth, Divine may he come
with all the Divine powers.

Rig Veda I.1.1, 5

Not what one knows with the mind, but that by
which the seers declare the mind is known. This
is the reality that you should know, not what
people regard as an object in this world.

Kena Upanishad I.5

Introduction to Vedanta

$\left(\text{T}\right)$ he first teachers who brought Yoga to the West came with the profound teachings of Vedanta as their greatest treasure to share with the world. They presented Vedanta as the philosophy of Self-realization and Yoga as the methodology by which to achieve it. Such great masters began with Swami Vivekananda at the end of the nineteenth century and continued with Swami Rama Tirtha, Paramahansa Yogananda, and the many disciples of Swami Shivananda of Rishikesh. They called their teaching *Yoga-Vedanta,* which they viewed as a complete science of spiritual growth.

However, in the course of time *asana* or yoga postures gained more popularity in the physically-minded West, and the Vedantic aspect of the teachings fell to the sidelines, particularly over the last twenty years. The result is that today few American Yoga teachers know what Vedanta is or can explain it to others. If they have an interest in meditation they generally look to Zen or Vipassana, not knowing that meditation is the very foundation of classical Yoga and its related traditions.

Even students of related disciplines like Ayurveda or Vedic astrology may know little about Vedanta, the path of self-knowledge that is the spiritual support and goal of these systems. Meanwhile, those who study the great Vedantic gurus of modern India, like Ramana Maharshi or Nisargadatta Maharaj, generally look at the particular teacher as the source of the teachings, and they may fail to understand the tradition that they are part of. In this way the heart teachings of India's great sages have become progressively lost even to those who claim to follow their teachings in the West.

The great sages of modern India were all Vedantins. Most notable is Ramana Maharshi, who emphasized the non-dualistic form of Vedanta and lived a life of direct Self-realization. Ramakrishna, Aurobindo, Anandamayi Ma, Nityananda, and Neem Karoli Baba, to mention but a few, were Vedantins, using the Vedantic terminology of Self-realization and God-realization. Vedantic traditions remain strong throughout India today, including many great teachers—for example, the different Shankaracharyas, who have never come to the West and are almost unknown here.

Current major teachers from India like Ma Amritanandamayi (Ammachi) and Satya Sai Baba similarly use the language of Vedanta and its emphasis on the Self. Maharishi Mahesh Yogi's Transcendental Meditation follows a Vedantic view of consciousness and cosmic evolution. Swami Rama, the founder of the Himalayan Institute, was another important Vedantic teacher in America. The main Hatha Yoga teachers in recent times, like Krishnamacharya of Madras or B.K.S. Iyengar, follow Vedantic teachings for the higher aspects of Yoga. Devotional approaches like the Hari Krishna movement reflect Vedantic devotional teachings. Without an understanding of Vedanta, therefore, it is difficult to understand these great teachers or their words to us.

The Philosophy of Vedanta

Vedanta is a simple philosophy. It says that our true Self, what it calls the *Atman,* is God. "I am God" *(aham brahmasmi)* is the supreme truth. The same consciousness that resides at the core of our being pervades the entire universe. To know ourselves is to know God and to become one with all. Vedanta is a philosophy of Self-realization, and its practice is a way of Self-realization through yoga and meditation.

Vedanta has a theistic side, recognizing a cosmic creator *(Ishvara)* who rules over the universe through the law of karma. God is the supreme teacher, the highest guru from whom all true teachings arise by the power of the divine word. Vedantic theism takes many forms such as the worship of Shiva, Vishnu, and the

Goddess. In fact, it can accommodate almost any form of theism that accepts karma and rebirth.

But in non-dualistic (Advaita) Vedanta, the Creator is not the ultimate reality. The ultimate reality is the Absolute, called *Brahman,* which transcends time, space and causation, standing above any personal creator. Our individual Self or soul *(Atman)* is one with the Absolute or Brahman, which is the supreme Self *(Paramatman).* The soul is not merely a part of the Creator but is one with the ground of Being-Consciousness-Bliss from which even the Creator arises.

Because of its emphasis on the Self and its recognition of many forms of theism, Vedanta lies behind the tolerance and syncretic tendency that exists in the Hindu religion. Because Hindus see religion as a vehicle for Self-knowledge they can accept many different sages, holy books and spiritual paths both inside their traditions and outside of them. Hinduism has always defined itself as *Sanatana Dharma,* "the universal or eternal dharma", which encompasses all dharmas and all possible spiritual paths. Many systems of Vedanta exist as well, with various philosophical differences among them covering all major views of God and consciousness. Vedanta, therefore, is not a closed but an open system that honors the Self in all beings and does not reduce it to any particular formula, personality or dogma.

> **"I am God" is the supreme truth.**

Vedanta is the oldest and most enduring spiritual teaching in India. It is fully emergent in the *Upanishads* and synthesized in the *Bhagavad Gita.* But it has ancient antecedents in Vedic literature, which recent archaeological finds now date to 3500 BCE, when the ancient Indus-Saraswati culture flourished throughout North India. The main terms and practices of Vedanta exist already in the cryptic *mantras* of the ancient *Vedas* that go back to the dawn of recorded history.

Reflecting the inner truth of the ancient *Vedas,* Vedanta is perhaps the oldest and most enduring spiritual teaching in the world. Spirituality, after all, is a pursuit of self-knowledge, not merely religious ritual or philosophy. Vedanta is the most characteristic philosophy of India and pervades most of the teachings of the land. Even modern movements like Sikh Dharma reflect the Vedantic idea that the individual soul is one with God.

Vedanta literally means "the end of the *Vedas*" but more appropriately it refers to the essence of the *Vedas*. From the standpoint of great yogis like Sri Aurobindo, the *Vedas* present the truth of Vedanta in a poetic-mantric language, while Vedanta presents Vedic mantric knowledge in the form of a rational philosophy. The wisdom hidden in the mantras of the ancient Rishis shines forth in the clear insight approaches of Vedanta.

Vedanta in the form of the early *Upanishads* preceded Buddhism by some centuries in India, perhaps by over a thousand years. Vedanta and Buddhism have much in common as ways of spiritual knowledge born of the Indic tradition. Many scholars see Buddhism as a modification of Vedanta, while others see it as a revolt against Vedanta. Vedanta eventually absorbed Buddhism in India, which by the seventh century had ceased to be a major religion in the country. Vedantic teachers accepted the figure of the Buddha as an incarnation *(avatara)* of Lord Vishnu, like Rama and Krishna, but rejected portions of Buddhist philosophy, particularly its denial of the existence of a creator.

Vedanta and Buddhism share ideas of karma, rebirth, and release from the cycle of rebirth *(samsara)*. They have similar practices of mantra and meditation. They follow the same ethical disciplines of non-violence *(ahimsa)* and vegetarianism, and both religious systems have well-developed monastic orders. Relative to their views of truth, the Mahayana form of Buddhism and Advaita (non-dualistic) Vedanta have a similar emphasis on the Absolute and regard the phenomenal world as maya or illusion.

Like Zen Buddhism, non-dualistic Vedanta emphasizes the Self or Self-nature as the supreme Reality. It honors that Self in the world of nature; thus its great Swamis retire into the forests for a life of meditation. Vedantic teachers laud the great beauty of nature, revealed through mountains such as the Himalaya, as reflections of our true being beyond the illusions of the world.

Vedantic Meditation

Dhyana, the Sanskrit term for meditation used by Hindus and Buddhists alike, first arises in Vedic literature. The *Upanishads* say, "By the Yoga of meditation (Dhyana Yoga) the sages saw the Divine Self-power, hidden in its own qualities" (*Shvetasvatara Upanishad* I.2). Another *Upanishad* states, "Meditate on Om as the Self" (*Katha Upanishad* II.5), showing the technique of *mantra* meditation.

Perhaps the most eloquent explication of meditation occurs in the *Chandogya,* one of the oldest *Upanishads.* "Meditation (Dhyana) indeed is greater than the mind. The earth as it were meditates. The atmosphere as it were meditates. Heaven as it were meditates. The waters as it were meditate. The mountains as it were meditate. Both men and gods as it were meditate. He who worships God (Brahman) as meditation, as far as meditation extends, so far does he gain the power to act as he wills" (*Chandogya Upanishad* VII.7).

According to Vedanta, liberation can be achieved only through spiritual knowledge, which requires meditation. Other factors, such as good works or rituals, are merely aids in the process. But such liberating knowledge is not any ordinary or conceptual knowledge. It is direct insight into one's own nature of pure consciousness.

Vedanta's main approach is threefold: hearing the teaching with a receptive mind *(shravana),* deep thinking about it *(manana),* and meditating on it consistently *(nididhyasana)* until full realization dawns, which is a state of *samadhi* or transcendent awareness. Such hearing is not simply noting the words of the teachings; it involves a deep inner listening with an open mind and heart. Such thinking requires full concentration and a firm intent to understand oneself. Such meditation is a repeated practice of self-examination and self-remembrance throughout the day as one's primary mental state.

Vedanta is a yoga of knowledge or a path of meditation. But it recognizes that other yogic paths are helpful, if not indispensable adjuncts, particularly the path of devotion *(Bhakti*

Yoga), which takes us directly to the Divine presence in the heart. Vedanta employs all the limbs of classical yoga from asana to samadhi, using all methods of the yogas of knowledge, devotion, service and technique, depending upon the needs of the student.

Generally Vedanta does not prescribe any particular form of meditation *en masse* or give the same technique to everyone. Emphasizing the Self, it recommends different methods relative to the level and temperament of each person and according to his or her unique nature and life circumstances. For this reason Vedantic meditation is hard to characterize and defies any stereotype. There is no standard formula for it. However, there are a number of common approaches, particularly the practice of Self-inquiry that this book highlights. Yet Self-inquiry is also applied on an individual basis, in which its methods can vary greatly from one person to another.

There is no standard formula for Vedantic meditation.

Vedantic meditation is not only diverse but generally private, emphasizing individual practice more than group practice. Its model is the wandering *sadhu* in solitary retreat, rather than the monk in a big monastery. However, meditation sessions do occur as part of the *satsangs* or gatherings that are common in the tradition. These may extend over a period of days or weeks. Yet those participating in such sessions may practice different forms of meditation, based upon the specific instructions of their teachers.

Buddhist meditation aims to return to the natural state of the mind, which is regarded as the enlightened state. This occurs through negating the self or ego and awakening the Buddha-mind *(Bodhichitta)*. Vedanta, on the other hand, is based on a clear distinction between the mind *(manas)*, which is regarded as a product of ignorance or maya, and the Self (Atman), which transcends the mind. The Vedantic way is to dissolve the mind into the Self which is our true nature beyond the mind and its conditioning.

This Vedantic emphasis on the Self is perhaps its main characteristic, as well as its main difference from Buddhism. While Vedanta approaches pure awareness as the Self or Atman, Buddhism prefers the term *anatman* or non-self. This Vedantic emphasis on the Self finds an echo in Western mystical traditions like Gnosticism, which influenced early Christianity, and Islamic Sufism; all refer to God as the Self or the supreme I-am. This Western tradition of the Self dates at least back to the Biblical revelation of God as I-am-that-I-am to Moses, but it was generally obscured by a greater emphasis on monotheism as the highest truth. We also find such utterances of the Divine I am in pagan traditions, like those of the Celts, Greeks and Egyptians, which have many factors in common with Hinduism.

Vedanta's theism, honoring the Divine Father and Mother, is another point of difference from Buddhism, which does not recognize the existence of any Creator apart from karma. Vedantic theism has some connections with the theistic traditions of the West, though it is more diverse and gives a greater place to the Goddess.

With its theistic side Vedanta recognizes surrender to the Divine as a primary method of spiritual practice along with Self-inquiry. By surrender to the Divine within our hearts we can go beyond all our difficulties and limitations. Yet surrender, though easy to conceive, is also a difficult process because it requires giving up the ego and all of our fears and desires that go with it. To facilitate this way of surrender is added chanting of Divine names and other devotional forms of worship. These can also be practiced along with knowledge-oriented techniques like Self-inquiry.

In Vedanta we approach the Creator as a means of discovering our true Self, in which both the soul and God are one. Union with God is part of the process of Self-realization. The Deity worshipped is ultimately the same as oneself and we must come to see it in all beings. Until we see the Divine beloved within our own heart, our devotion has not yet reached its highest goal.

Vedanta postulates certain ultimate principles of the Absolute, God, the Soul, and Nature. It recognizes the supreme reality as

Being, Consciousness, and Bliss (called *Satchidananda*), which is eternal and infinite. In this regard Vedanta follows an idealistic philosophy much like the Greek philosophies of Plato, Plotinus or Parmenides. Part of Vedantic meditation is contemplating these higher principles—for example meditating, on the formless Absolute and its laws (dharmas) behind the world of nature.

Meditation on the oneness of all is another important Vedantic approach. Vedanta sees pure unity or oneness as the supreme principle in existence. It recognizes a single law or dharma governing the entire universe. Whatever we do to others we do to ourselves because there is really only one Self in all. This is also the basis of Vedantic ethics that emphasize non-violence and compassion, treating others not like our self but as our Self.

Vedantic meditation aims at returning us to this original state of unity, in which all beings abide in the Self within the heart. While Vedanta like Buddhism does recognize the Void, stating the Self is like space, it holds that the Self pervades even the Void and witnesses it. For this reason Vedanta seldom regards the Void as the ultimate principle and emphasizes the unity of Pure Being more than voidness.

Vedanta does not neglect the psychological side, either. Like most Indian spiritual systems, its purpose is to show us how to permanently overcome all suffering. Vedantic meditation involves meditating upon suffering and removing its cause. Vedanta regards ignorance of our true Self as the cause of all our life problems. Because we don't know our true Self, which is pure awareness beyond the body and mind, we must suffer, seeking to find happiness in the shifting external world. By returning to our true Self we can transcend psychological suffering and detach ourselves from any possible physical suffering as well. The pain of body and mind do not belong to the Self that is beyond time and space.

Vedanta has a profound understanding of the different layers and functions of the mind, from what we call the unconscious to the highest superconsciousness, for which it has a precise terminology. It recognizes the role of *samskaras,* the tendencies created in previous births, as causing our present condition and its difficulties as well as rewards. Vedanta sees fear and desire as the main roots of the mind that get us caught in the cycle of rebirth. It regards the ego or the false I, the I identified with the body, as the basis of these problems. Another part of Vedantic meditation is clearing our minds of the afflictions and karmic residues that block the practice of meditation. This involves affirming our true Self, which is the master of the Universe beyond all fear and desire, birth and death.

Vedanta recommends regular meditation for everyone, particularly during the hour or two before dawn, which it calls *Brahma Muhurta* or the hour of God. Sunrise and sunset are other important times for meditation because at these transitional periods in nature, energy can be more easily transformed. The times of the new, full and half moons are also excellent, as are the solstice and equinoctial points. Meditation is part of the very rhythm of life and nature and its ongoing transformations.

Very important for meditation is the period immediately before sleep in order to clear the day's karma from the mind. Vedanta regards the deep sleep state as the doorway to the Self, our natural daily return to God. Its practices develop our awareness through waking and dream to deep sleep and beyond. Deep sleep is the knot of ignorance; when it is removed through meditation, we can discover our true nature and eternal peace. Maintaining awareness through dream and deep sleep is an important and ancient Vedantic approach.

Vedanta is perhaps the world's oldest continuous meditation tradition. Like our eternal soul, it witnesses all the changes of time and history. It takes on new forms and inspires new teachers in every generation. Such an ancient and diverse meditation tradition is of great importance for all those who wish to understand what meditation really is and how best to practice it.

Self-Inquiry and Its Practice

T he practice of Self-inquiry, called *Atma-vichara* in Sanskrit, is the most important meditation practice in the Vedantic tradition. It is the main practice of the yoga of knowledge *(Jnana Yoga)*, which itself is traditionally regarded as the highest of the yogas because it takes us most directly to liberation.

Self-inquiry is the primary method through which Self-realization—the realization of our true nature beyond mind and body—is achieved. Self-inquiry is mainly known today through the teachings of Ramana Maharshi (1878-1950), who made this approach accessible to the general public, offering it to any individual who was capable of receiving the teaching. Traditionally, Self-inquiry was reserved mainly for monks *(Swamis)* who had renounced the world. A strong Self-inquiry tradition persists in the Swami orders of India today, particularly in the south of the country.

Yet Self-inquiry in some form or another can be helpful to all people at all stages of life, as part of everyone's quest for Self-realization. We all want to know ourselves and unfold our deeper potential in life. This requires understanding ourselves on all levels of body, mind and spirit, particularly the deepest level of the heart.

Technique of Self-Inquiry

Because the teaching of Self-inquiry is direct and simple, its literature is not as extensive as that of other yogic practices. In addition, the path of Self-inquiry demands a certain ripeness or readiness of mind that may require other practices to develop.

The process of Self-inquiry is so simple that it can be

explained in a few words. To practice it you need only trace the root of your thoughts back to the I-thought, from which all other thoughts arise. This is initiated by the question "Who am I?". By asking, "Who am I?" our thought current naturally gets focused on the search for the true Self and we forget about all other concerns and worries of the mind.

All our thoughts are based directly or indirectly on the thought of the self. Thoughts such as "Where am I going?" or "What will I do tomorrow?" are based directly on the self. Thoughts like "What will happen to my family?" or "Who will win the next election?" are based indirectly on the thought of the self because they refer ultimately to our own concerns.

Our thoughts consist of two components. The first is a subjective factor—I, me or mine. The second is an objective factor—a state, condition or object with which the I is involved, particularly the activities of our own body and mind. The habit of the mind is to get caught in the object portion and never look within to recognize the true Self apart from external concerns.

> The truth is that we don't know who we really are.

The result is that the pure I or the I-in-itself is unknown to us. What we call ourselves is but a conglomerate of "I am this" or "this is mine," in which the subject is confused with an object, quality or condition. Self-inquiry consists of discarding the object portion in order to discover the pure Subject. This requires withdrawing our attention from the objects of sensation, emotion and thought by discriminating these from the formless Self or seer that observes them.

The truth is that we don't know who we really are. What we call our Self is but some thought, emotion or sensation that we are temporarily identified with and that is constantly changing. Our lives are shrouded in ignorance about our true nature, springing from the most basic feelings that we have, especially our bodily identity. We are not the body. Rather, the body is a vehicle or vesture in which our true Self is obscured. As long as we don't question this process of self-identification we must come to sorrow and remain in darkness and confusion.

However, Self-inquiry does not consist of merely repeating the question "Who am I?" over and over again in our minds, which is only a tiring mental exercise. It means holding to the search for the true Self in all that one does. It requires that we have a real and fundamental doubt about who we are, through which we can reject all outer identifications. It is as if one had amnesia and didn't know who one was and had to give full attention to the matter before anything else could be done.

Self-inquiry, moreover, is not merely an intellectual or psychological inquiry but an inquiry with one's entire energy and attention. It requires a full and one-pointed concentration, not interrupted by the intrusion of other thoughts. The thought current naturally moves back to the Self to the extent that we do not preoccupy our minds with outside stimulation. The problem is that the senses present us with so many distractions that it is difficult to look within. Self-inquiry means to constantly question and reverse this process of extroversion by seeking out the origin of our awareness and energy in the heart.

True Self-inquiry is not just questioning the limitation of our outer identity, like our family, political or religious affiliation—whether one is a wife, a father, a Christian, a Hindu or an atheist. It questions our entire identity as an embodied being. It does not stop short with some general identity as a human, cosmic or spiritual being but rejects any formation of thought as our true nature. It directs us back to the pure "I" that is not identified with any form of objectivity, physical or mental.

The true Self is not only beyond human distinctions, it is beyond all divisions of time and space, name and form, birth and death. It is beyond all experience because it is the experiencer or observer of all. Self-inquiry leads us ultimately to the Absolute in which the phenomenal world becomes little more than a mirage of the mind and senses. It goes far beyond the discovery of some greater self, or any human or creative potential, to what is beyond all limitations. In the process we expand our sense of self to include the entire universe and all of its multifarious creatures.

Perhaps the easiest approach to Self-inquiry is what is called "discrimination between the seer and the seen." This can be outlined in a few easy steps.

- First, one discriminates the seer from the external objects in one's environment, which constantly change though the seer remains the same. For example, the eye is not blemished by imperfections in the objects that it sees.

- Second, one discriminates the seer from the sense organs. There are several senses and each varies in acuity, but the seer of the senses is constant and not altered by their fluctuations. For example, the mind can witness imperfections in the eye, like lack of acuity or blurring of vision.

- Third, one discriminates between the seer and mental states. Thoughts and feelings continually change but the seer, if we look deeply, remains the same. For example, the seer of anger does not cease to be when anger itself passes away.

- Fourth, one discriminates between the seer and the ego, between the pure-I and the I identified with body, emotion or thought. Then the pure Self devoid of external associations can shine forth. For example, we can witness our ego states like pride and dejection, just as we can observe shifting sensations or emotions.

- Fifth, one abides in the pure Self devoid of objectivity, letting all the contents of the mind come and go like waves and bubbles on the sea.

It is best to do this process by degrees, taking one's time at each stage. All is contained in the fifth state of abiding as the seer. When we return to the state of the seer, all that we see merges back into the light of seeing, revealing its nature as pure consciousness.

Self-Inquiry and Other Meditation Practices

Self-inquiry is a kind of mental activity, though of a special nature. It is not an attempt to suppress thought or to hold the mind in an empty state, like certain formless meditation approaches. Self-inquiry does not teach that all thinking is bad but holds that one type of thinking is necessary for liberation. It teaches us to use the mind in the right way, which is to turn it into a tool of inquiry, rather than a means of enjoyment as we ordinarily use it. This requires a revolution in the nature of the mind, awakening an inner intelligence to counter the outgoing desire-based mind.

The practice of Self-inquiry requires a great deal of thoughtfulness, particularly in its preliminary phases, along with the development of a strong mental discipline. It requires that we seriously think about who we are and what we are doing in life. Unless we have resolved our problems through deep examination and observation (which is the first stage of Samadhi), it is useless, not to mention impossible, to silence the mind (which comes at the second stage of Samadhi).

Yet such inquiry is thinking born of awareness. It is not mere mechanical thinking or speculative thought. One could say it is the true thinking that arises from a mind no longer dominated by the burden of memory. It is more akin to observation than to any discursive activity.

One may ask how Self-inquiry, a mental activity, can control or negate the mind? Does not mental activity only increase mental activity? The answer is that the mind cannot be quiet when its contents have not been released. Self-inquiry is the means of reversing the action of the mind, taking it back to inaction, which itself must begin as an action. It is reversing the thought current to return to the ocean of thought-free awareness, in which the mind's activity naturally comes to an end. We must go to the root of something in order to change it. Mental activity springs from a source, the "I-thought." We return to the I-thought in order to go beyond all other thoughts.

Self-inquiry, therefore, is not simply a kind of mindfulness in which we focus on being aware of something, like our breath, our hands or a particular activity that we may be doing. Self-inquiry does not say "Be aware of your breath" but rather "Who is breathing?" or "Who is really alive?". It does not say "Be mindful of your body" but rather asks "Are you the body?". Self-inquiry is not a form of passive or choiceless awareness, but has a dynamic and probing energy. It questions the validity of the entity who thinks that he is aware. It does not accept our awareness as it is but asks "Who is aware?" "What is the nature of this awareness?". Self-inquiry uses the energy of observation but as a tool of questioning, ever taking it to a deeper level of examination.

> **Who is aware? What is the nature of this awareness?**

Similarly, Self-inquiry is not a form of concentration in which we try to focus exclusively on one object, like a *mantra,* to the exclusion of all other thoughts. It is concentration on the Self, where our attention automatically returns whatever else we may try to do. We cannot completely concentrate on anything else unless we first know ourselves. Otherwise the I-thought must arise and break the continuity of our concentration. Rather than fighting the I-thought and trying to return to another object of concentration, Self-inquiry concentrates on the I-thought to put an end to other thoughts.

Self-inquiry is also not a form of contemplation, in which we think about or mentally reflect upon some object or idea. It is not the contemplation of guru, mantra or chakra, a great idea like Oneness, or even God. It is not using the mind to think about something, but using the thought process to question itself. It does not ask, "What is God?" but looks to the Divine within us, the Self as God. It says, "If God is apart from the Self, then of what use is God?" If God is not apart from the Self then we can best find it through the Self.

Self-inquiry is not an attempt to be good or to make ourselves better either. It is not a form of self-improvement or a means of gaining religious merit. It is questioning the reality of the entity that we think is either good or bad, that can either improve or degenerate. It questions our efforts to be this or that and says that without knowing ourselves it is of no lasting benefit to try to become anything, however great or noble.

Similarly, Self-inquiry is not an attempt to make the world better or to bring love or compassion into the world. It is a questioning whether what we call the world has any reality at all, or is just a reflection of our thought process. Yet Self-inquiry brings us into contact with our true Self that is one with all. This is the basis of all compassion and real service in the world, which transcend thought and selfish motivation.

While Self-inquiry leads to the absolute truth, which can be called the pure-I or Self, the name is only a pointer. One can call it God, knowledge, enlightenment, Buddha or whatever one likes, but it is not a state that can be defined according to an idea, or in which mental recognition can occur. Self-inquiry is not seeking any mental answer and has no conceptual result. It questions the validity of all entities and conclusions created by the mind.

Self-inquiry is a provocative state that directs awareness to its core in the heart. It is like a sword that cuts through everything. It does not even allow us to hold to a happy or peaceful state of consciousness short of real Self-realization. It does not allow us to rest content in the contemplation of objects, principles or ideas, however lofty these may be.

This does not mean that such practices as mindfulness, concentration or contemplation are not useful, that ethical disciplines are not necessary, or that mantra, *pranayama* or the study of spiritual teachings do not have their place. It only means that these are support practices for Self-inquiry or an alternative line of approach. To follow ethical disciplines, to place the body in a comfortable position, to deepen the breath, to withdraw the mind from sensory stimulation, to develop concentration and other yogic practices, all should be done, but we must not stop there; we must proceed to Self-inquiry. Only a rare individual can proceed directly to Self-inquiry without such support practices, and even he or she can benefit greatly from them.

Simple formless Self-inquiry is difficult to sustain, except among advanced aspirants who have well-developed powers of attention and dispassion from all external objects starting with the body itself. Such detachment is, of course, extremely rare in this materialistic and sensate age. Additional practices are usually necessary to build the competence for this effort, which is said to be as daunting as scaling the steep rock face of a high mountain.

The general rule is that if the mind is not in a *sattvic* or clear state then Self-inquiry cannot be properly pursued. The sattvic mind is the mind characterized by peace, devotion, compassion, purity and wisdom, as well as freedom from imagination, desire, anger and animosity. All yogic practices help develop such a sattvic mind. If the mind is dulled through wrong food, sexual indulgence, disturbed sensory or mental activities and entertainments, including worry, anxiety, ambition or pride it will not have the acuity to truly practice Self-inquiry. The mind must be as sharp as the edge of a razor. Otherwise it will not be subtle enough to reach the core of thought.

Guidelines to Practice

Self-inquiry can be done at all times, in all places and circumstances. It does not require knowledge of special yoga techniques, though these can be helpful aids. It does not require that we otherwise try to overtly change ourselves or what we are doing in life. Self-inquiry only requires that we place our attention on the source from which thought naturally springs, which is the I-thought. This, however, is one of the most difficult of all things because it requires control of the wavering and fickle mind and senses.

It is easiest to practice Self-inquiry when we are sitting alone, particularly in nature. The outer world of nature is the door to our inner nature. It provides the space and peace that allow the mind to return to its source. In nature, apart from personal involvements and social stresses, we can easily inquire into who we really are—the real nature of the seer. We should do this on a regular basis. Self-inquiry is like sitting on a high mountain peak, touching space and contemplating the world of the senses below.

We can practice Self-inquiry when we are around other people or even during our work, but it requires more effort because social contact pulls the mind outward. It is important therefore to reduce our outer activities and social contacts to aid in the process of Self-inquiry. Yet when people come together specifically to pursue spiritual practices—called *satsanga* or communion with the wise—such social contact is a powerful aid to practice. Such contact magnetizes our higher thoughts, feelings and aspirations. Communion among practitioners is always encouraged, including study, dialogue and meditation together, especially with a good teacher or realized guru.

To practice Self-inquiry while we are engaged in action, it helps to call to mind the inquiry "Who is the doer?". In this way we will not let our actions dominate our awareness. Our actions will become a form of *Karma Yoga* or a path of Divine service.

> **Even a beginner can benefit from the practice of Self-inquiry.**

Even a beginner can benefit from the practice of Self-inquiry. It is not difficult to start the process of Self-inquiry and experience a shift in our sense of self. Our thoughts begin to subside as we realize that what we have called our self is largely only an identification of the I with some thought or feeling that is external and transient. We see that the more our thoughts deviate from Self-awareness, the more confusion and suffering are created for us.

Yet though this process is not difficult to initiate, it is very difficult to sustain for long periods of time. Some have questioned whether Self-inquiry can become a constant practice at all, or whether it is something that one really does only once, at the right moment that has been prepared for by one's entire life.

Most of us will discover that we can practice Self-inquiry for a time, perhaps extending through several months, but it is hard to maintain it as a primary or ongoing practice. It is not a practice like pranayama or mantra that can be done in a routine manner. There is no particular structure or ceremony to it. It is not a step-by-step process with different levels and angles that can be easily mapped out and explored. It remains at the center but to get to the center, and stay there is not easy. While we may find we can make some headway with it, we often reach a barrier that is hard to cross. While it is easy to get rid of superficial identifications like those of a political or social nature, it is much more difficult to really break our identification with our own body, emotions and memories.

Self-inquiry is a difficult practice to judge one's progress in. Because it has no real stages, one can wonder whether one is making any progress at all, or one can imagine great progress when there is really none. The easiest way to determine one's progress is by one's detachment, peace and equanimity of mind. If one is going deeply into the practice one will experience a state of samadhi in which one goes beyond body and ego-consciousness; the ordinary mind dissolves and time and space disappear. Yet false samadhis can occur in which some aspect of the ego remains and distorts higher experiences, which is why the guidance of a genuine teacher remains important.

Such a true teacher understands all sides of the teaching and its support disciplines and can judge the specific level and temperament of each student. This type of person, however, is not easy to find. True teachers of Self-inquiry are often reclusive and seldom take on large numbers of students, and usually only those who are ready for intense practice.

On the other hand, there are false or superficial teachers, purveyors of instant enlightenment, who breed confusion and often speak against preliminary practices, the place of which they do not understand. There are also well-intentioned but naïve teachers who overestimate their own attainments. They can introduce people to the practice but don't have the ability to take them to a really deep level.

The best judge of a good teacher is the peace that one feels in his or her presence. It is not their personal charisma or how high one feels around them, which can be factors of illusion. Also important is whether the teacher is part of a real lineage or tradition of Self-realization. Whether or not a teacher is recognized by respected Vedantic teachers in India today, where such traditions are alive, is perhaps the best indication. Anyone can claim to be enlightened or Self-realized, which is more an inner than an outer state, so one should always be careful in choosing a teacher.

Finding the question "Who am I?" to be too direct, simple or monotonous, some of us may try other questions like "What is fear?" or "What are we really seeking in life?". Much of the teaching of J. Krishnamurti consists of this type of inquiry that is not as pointed as Self-inquiry and offers several angles of approach that can lead in the same direction. Yet even this more diverse type of inquiry may not be easy to sustain over time. It also can deviate more easily from the center and end in psychological analysis or another purely mental process. We should aim such questioning back to the Self for it to be truly efficacious.

Most of us fail at Self-inquiry for two reasons: either we haven't prepared the ground for it properly, or we haven't been consistent in our practice. While such an instant enlightenment pat—becoming immediately the Self of all—is an appealing idea that can arouse a temporary enthusiasm, it may require lifetimes, not merely years of deep practice to succeed. Therefore, it is best to approach Self-inquiry not as a means of sudden realization, but as a life long process. One should first aim at a regular practice—for example, half an hour morning and evening after other yogic practices to prepare the mind—and continue this for some time before judging the success of one's endeavors.

Many great teachers, like Swami Shivananda of Rishikesh, emphasized including Self-inquiry along with an integral yogic practice of devotion, mantra, asana and pranayama. He used to say that if an unprepared person asked the question "Who am I?", the answer is "only the same old fool." Even Ramana Maharshi, though he mainly taught Self-inquiry, encouraged such support practices and never spoke against their usefulness. The traditional path of Self-inquiry follows from a well-rounded spiritual life, but this is not so appealing to those of us today who come from a non-devotional and anti-discipline cultural background that wants immediate results. For this reason we must approach Self-inquiry with patience and perseverance, looking up to the Absolute but sure of the earth on which we stand.

In the ultimate truth the Self is the only reality. Our inquiry into it and all else that we do is merely a fiction of thought. Yet this fiction of thought is not personal but includes the entire universe. It consists of all possible types of mental activity, conscious and subconscious. The world is the great maya or illusion of the Lord *(Bhagavan)* that requires not only our own selfless effort but Divine grace in order to cross. Yet attempting this is the real purpose of our birth and the real goal of all our lifetimes. Let us seek our true Self with honesty and humility, and all the wonders of the universe and what is beyond must come to us.

PART II

The Challenges of Awareness

Far apart, opposite and contrary are the
Knowledge and the Ignorance.

Dwelling in the midst of Ignorance, thinking
themselves to be wise, the foolish totter like the
blind led by the blind. The higher goal does not
appeal to these heedless children, deluded by the
material world.

Katha Upanishad II.4

The Creator opened the gates of the senses to
look without, not to see the inner Self. Only a
rare sage with his eye turned within, desiring
immortality, sees the inner Self.

The childish follow after outer desires and enter
into the noose extended by death.

Katha Upanishad IV.1

In this section we will explore some of the main issues of the
spiritual path from a Vedantic view, in a practical and non-tech-
nical manner. Each short topic, arranged in alphabetical order,
addresses an important concern of the spiritual life and provides
a different angle of approach to it.

Action and Transformation

Our actions are based on the seeking of results. We are engaged in a process of causation, trying to produce one thing through another. Such action is, in a sense, dishonest. We are doing one thing only to arrive at something else. The result is more important than our regard for what we are actually doing.

We seldom do anything for its own sake. Our action is not direct and present. It follows an ulterior motivation and a looking to the future. Our action works through time, which is the past and the future, and the denial of the present that is awareness. Action that seeks a result, therefore, creates bondage to time. It attaches us to the stream of causation, in which we ourselves, becoming part of the process, can be moved, influenced and manipulated according to that which we seek.

Matter, time, space and causation are ultimately the same. We see matter, an inert or raw material to be used, according to our seeking of results. To seek results is to create matter, to turn things into manipulatable objects. For example, if I desire to become a political leader, I must learn how to use the masses of people in order to give me power and influence. I must turn them into a tool and mold them like clay according to my ambition, which is exactly what most of our leaders attempt. In that seeking of results, I turn living human beings into mere instruments for arriving at what I want. Were I not seeking anything, I could look at people directly as human beings. When we see others as human beings, as ourselves, we cannot manipulate them.

Causation, the seeking of results, removes us from the present and ties us to a future based upon the past (the past being our desire and the future its fulfillment). This binds us to a mentality of absence and want. Turning the world (which is also our inmost self) into an object alienates us and creates division in space. The seeking of results binds us to time, space and karma, not as some metaphysical theory but as a psychological fact. It creates our false world-idea based upon the ego, the world of sorrow and confusion or samsara that is the denial of our true self and being.

From the ego, which is the central focus of the ignorance, the original fissure in consciousness between self and other, comes our entire bondage to time, space and causation. Apart from the seeking of results, all life is spiritual, sacred or Nirvanic—a pure and inviolable existence.

Addiction and Thought

O ur lives are based upon a lack of attention that reflects a deeper spiritual ignorance. We spend our time pursuing the things of the world, thinking they will make us happy. This ignorance is essentially a preoccupation with ourselves—who we are, what we want, where we are going and so on. Out of this self-focus we create various attractions and repulsions, likes and dislikes, loves and hates. In this process we become attached to what gives us pleasure or happiness. This causes some form of addiction, which is nothing but a dependency on something external to fulfill us.

Most of us have many addictions, which we may call habits and interests, or even skills and talents. Such addictions as drugs, alcohol or gambling are but the most evident forms of the addictive pattern of our entire behavior. Some of us are addicted to sex, others to food, others to business, to knowledge, or even to religious practices. Whatever we become dependent on to occupy our time or fill our minds is a kind of addiction. All external seeking—whether for pleasure, wealth, status or knowledge—is not ultimately different from an alcoholic looking for a drink.

> **Thought is our most basic addiction.**

Thought is our most basic addiction from which all other addictions derive like branches. Thought is a habit, an unconscious mechanism of the mind. If you do not believe this, then try to control your thoughts, try to stop thinking. Obviously thought is not a conscious process but a compulsion. We automatically think about ourselves and what we will get in life. As long as we are ruled by this stream of mechanical thought we are addicts of one type or another, and our addiction must distort our perception.

The addiction to thought is, of course, extremely difficult to transcend. It is much more fundamental than any other addiction and is their root. Only if we think repeatedly about something will we become addicted to it. As long as we accept the addiction of thought, we place ourselves in a life of unconsciousness, inertia and dependency. Only if we counter this mental inertia with the energy of consciousness can we become free of addiction. This requires redirecting our mental attention to inquiry and meditation.

Do we really want to live asleep, to be creatures of habit compelled by external forces and artificially induced needs? Can such a life ever bring us truth or happiness? The only way to wake up is to recognize that we are asleep. The real way to get beyond addiction is to question its origin in the separate self.

Anxiety and Its Message

F ear and anxiety shadow our lives. Anxiety, we could say, is the very way of our culture. We are made impressionable to it at a young age as a means of social control. Anxiety takes many forms, like the anxiety to be loved, the anxiety to be happy, to be well off or to become somebody. And there is the anxiety of possible loss that breeds insurance companies and churches. We invent all kinds of guarantees and securities to protect us. And yet there is no end to our anxiety.

It is no wonder that we are anxious. We have based our mentality on the outer factors of life that are intrinsically uncertain and unreliable. As long as we are caught in outward seeking, we must suffer anxiety. We are always trying to figure things out, to plan and control them, to make them go our way or to bring us what we want. The very action of thought must result in anxiety because life is beyond our control. Even when we succeed in getting what we want, we find that it is really not what we thought it would be. Our effort to control life and plan the future separates us from life's beneficence. In trying to take care of ourselves, we lose the care of life and cease to care for life. As there is no reality to sustain us except what we create by our own personal and collective efforts in the face of the unknown, we find anxiety lurking everywhere.

For most of us there is no overcoming anxiety; there is only its postponement or its palliation. Anxiety is the inevitable effect of the way we live, and the effect cannot be removed without the eradication of its cause. Non-surrender to life, non-perception of truth, and the imposing of our personal will upon existence must cause anxiety. Our isolated center of separate existence, the personal self or ego, is a constriction of energy, an alienation from life that must remain problematical and uncertain.

Anxiety is evidence that our lives are out of harmony with reality. We should feel anxious, because we are placing our sense of reality in the petty and the fleeting. Letting anxiety unfold its significance through meditation will reveal to us all the illusions of the mind. The problem is not anxiety itself but dependence on thought that breeds anxiety, our attachment to the self that is ever in turmoil. Anxiety is a mirror in which the inadequacy of the separate self is revealed. We should not destroy the mirror but understand its message.

Anxiety is evidence that our lives are out of harmony with reality.

Each thing is teaching us the truth of what we are. Pain and anxiety reveal how we create sorrow for ourselves. They are friends exposing the error of our ways. There is no escape from them unless we recognize what they reveal to us.

Being

$\left(\text{B}\right)$ eing, truth, God or whatever name one may give to Reality, is not a thing of thought. It is not the content of any conceptual knowledge and cannot be comprehended by any mental process however subtle or synthetic. It is entirely outside the domain of the mind, memory and sensation. Being is not in the known and the thinkable and cannot be arrived at through extending their fields. It can only be approached through the abandonment and surrender of the mind and its assertions.

The mind cannot know being or reality. It can only know the appearance of name, form and becoming. It cannot know the essence of anything, whether a rock, a tree, a person or an emotion. It cannot touch the presence which is sacred, only the surface details of life. Living as we do in thought, we cannot know reality, though we may think about it in many different ways.

The mind itself has no true reality, existence or being. The separate self is a problematical entity, ever trying to be, endlessly becoming, but never arriving at a state of lasting peace or fullness. The mind has only thought, name and form—a superficial knowledge caught between two greater ignorances of birth and death. It is never present, never simply existent or in unity with all. It is always absent, elsewhere, isolated in its pattern of seeking and trying to be. The mind is too complicated and jaded by sensation and memory to know the simplicity and innocence of the sacred. It pursues differences of form and misses the space of being that is equal in all.

Whatever we think about is not the reality. Whoever we think about, once we have formed an image or identity, is not the real person or conscious subject. The real being, which is one in all, cannot be reduced to a pattern of thought or emotion but can only be communed with in receptivity and silence. Being is ever responsive to us, but closed as we are in our thought processes we cannot know it. Being is openness and beneficence that over-flows from the timeless into creation.

We do not perceive this extraordinary reality because our attention is elsewhere. We miss it because we are involved in the distractions of our own thought-patterns. Being is self-luminous and self-revealing, but because we are hypnotized by our own personal becoming we cannot discover its presence. The screen of our self-centered thoughts blocks us from it.

To know being we must first be. Only being can know being. We are That by what we are, not by what we seek or what we desire. We become That by our no longer striving to become something else. This is offering the mind into the flame of aware-ness that delivers us beyond time and sorrow.

Beyond Self-Illusion

T o discover the truth we must first have no illusions about ourselves. The first illusion we must overcome is the idea that we don't have any illusions about ourselves. Our entire identity is an illusion sustained by our thoughts and emotions and their assertions and defenses.

We must realize that we are capable of projecting every sort of illusion. Projecting illusions does not require any special or overt process but is inherent in our very way of thinking. All thought is based on the "I," the ego, and naturally places our self and its concerns at the center. As long as we do not question our thought process we must project some illusion of self-importance: that we are great, good, wise, holy, talented, beautiful and so on. This is but the naïve egoism of thought and matter, its localization of reality into its narrow sphere of time and space.

What makes us susceptible to illusion is the subtlety and depth of the drive to become somebody. Our own thoughts, which reflect the ego, tend to magnify us. Environmental influences manipulate us through playing on our desires. All this breeds illusion and confines us to limitation because self-importance is but glorifying ourselves as material objects.

It is impossible to avoid having illusions about ourselves, which are inherent in the ways of thought. We must observe these for what they are. Illusion is inherent in matter's limitation of form, but we do not have to be deluded by it any more than we are deluded into thinking a nearby tree is larger than a distant mountain. We must have perspective in our awareness, a detached observation, understanding the limitations of the mind as well as the senses.

The Consumer
and the Consumed

T he materialism of modern culture is nowhere more evident than in our consumer-oriented society. Most of the time we function as consumers, taking some product from the external world and using it up. We are not creators, but spectators and consumers of things given to us from the outside.

We are consumers not only in the material realm with food, clothes, cars and new relationships, but also in the intellectual and spiritual realms, with new books, tapes and seminars. We bring the consumer mentality wherever we go. All consumption is a kind of eating, in which we ingest some product from the external world. In the process we become more material, heavy, dense and dependent.

The consumer is the consumed. To be a consumer is to be involved in a process of destruction. Consumption occurs as the inertia of matter feeding on itself. Eventually we ourselves are thrown away like yesterday's newspaper. In the process of consuming things, our life and creativity are eaten up by commercial forces and worldly interests. We take in temporary sensations or ideas that keep us distracted, removed from our true Self and its nobler aspirations.

We project this consumer-oriented mentality into the spiritual world. We try to get the right spiritual information, go to the right places and experience the right things in order to consume our way to God or enlightenment. The ego is the consumer. Consumption is the logic of the material ego to feed itself, expand and grow. To be a consumer is the most primitive level of being. It is to be a mouth, an eater, a devourer of things. It is not to see, but to eat or be eaten.

To discover the truth of who we are, we must discard the consumer mentality and reclaim our spiritual dignity as detached observers. Our true being is in consciousness. It is immaterial, empty of things, devoid of all that is outer. Our true nature cannot be arrived at through any form of consumption but only by allowing ourselves to be consumed by it.

> **The consumer is the consumed.**

The Eternal

For most of us the eternal is a vague idea, distant and unattainable, quite apart from the real things of the temporal world that we experience n our daily lives. Yet if we look deeply, the transient is illusory, not the eternal.

The observer is different from the observed. The subject is not an object. The characteristics of the seer are different from those of the seen. The eye is not blemished by imperfections in the objects that it perceives.

Similarly, the consciousness that observes time is not itself of time. To perceive the transient, consciousness must be eternal. We are always in the eternal. Thought creates the idea of our being in time, but awareness itself is beyond all change and fluctuation. The real present is of the eternal; it is not the constantly changing moments that we experience through the windows of the mind.

It is not difficult to step out of time and find the eternal. Whenever we cease to identify ourselves with external objects, our awareness naturally returns to its eternal equipoise. We continually experience things as beginning and ending. This shows that our consciousness itself does not begin or end. Yet instead of opening up to this natural wisdom of eternity, we try to find something lasting in external objects, which only breeds sorrow. To find the eternal we need only give up our seeking in the realm of time.

Time itself is an escape from the eternal. A return to the eternal is the death of time, which is the mind. However much we immerse ourselves in time, it must come to an end, and all that we succeed in avoiding is the Divine.

Fear and the Unknown

Most of us are afraid of the unknown. Yet if we look deeply we will see that this is an illusion. We cannot really be afraid of something if we don't know what it is. What we are actually afraid of is that the unknown is something that we already know and don't like.

We cannot really be afraid of death because we don't know what it is. Behind our fear of death is the pain of losing our connection to what we already know and are attached to. What we are afraid of is pain, suffering and loneliness. We are only afraid of the unknown because we think that it will make us feel bad.

The real cause of pain, which we should seek to remove, is our clinging to the transient things. Pain is bred by attachment to the known, which must pass away. Only by removing that attachment can the cause of pain be eliminated. Attachment to the known creates the fear of the unknown, but what we fear in the unknown is just the pain and sorrow of the known.

All the things that we fear in life—pain, unhappiness, loneliness and poverty—have an inner teaching for us. They point out the limited nature of our seeking. Attached to the known and the transient, we must feel fear. Fear is telling us that our idea of reality is limited and unreal, that it is uncertain and must come to an end. Fear reveals that the way we think is blind and self-centered.

> **Most of us are afraid of the unknown.**

Fear is the nature of the mind that is attached to the self and its precarious boundaries. The ending of fear comes when we cease seeking fulfillment in the outer world, when we merge the world into our hearts through the power of self-vision. Giving up the known takes us beyond fear and makes death into liberation.

The Guru's Role

S piritual teachings emphasize the role of the guru or spiritual teacher and define it in different ways. While the guru function is ultimately an inner reality, it works through various human teachers in the outer world. The true guru is the guiding intelligence of life behind the veil of thought. When we are no longer thinking about the world and its objects, this guiding intelligence manifests and points the way to truth.

The mind reflects the external world. We create an image of ourselves as a person in the world. When we come into contact with a real human guru, he or she can reflect back to us the world of reality. The guru mirrors back not our image as a bodily identity, but the pure consciousness hidden deep inside us. This self-mirroring process radically changes the idea of who we are and reveals our true nature. This is the true meaning of "seeing the guru", which is the same as seeing our Self. Therefore, while the real guru is ultimately not a mere human person, contacting the guru consciousness through a human teacher is a great aid and catalyst to connect us to it. Merely imagining a guru inside does not have this potential transformative power.

Yet there is no real conflict between seeking out genuine teachers and self-reliantly seeking the truth. Just as the student who studies on his own is more likely to gain additional help from his teachers, so true guidance comes more easily to those who are already striving on their own. We must be receptive to guidance if we are to learn in any field of life. This brings us into contact with various teachers and teachings, outwardly or inwardly, of the past or the present, who can be instrumental in changing our consciousness.

Following a guru is primarily a matter of practice and should not be confused with a mere adulation of personalities. Putting up a teacher's picture on our wall doesn't change how we perceive ourselves. The true guru is not a mere person or body but represents the formless truth. Without living according to their teachings we are not truly following the teacher.

The best way to respect the words of wisdom imparted by spiritually realized souls is to put their teachings into practice in our daily lives. This is the real meaning of the guru as a presence in human society. We must honor the guru in both the outer world and the inner world, which is to live according to the laws of the sages.

Karma and Time

I n our deeper nature we are not under any necessary bondage to karma or destiny. As spiritual beings, we are inherently free of time and its compulsions. In the present moment all is open, free and creative. Nor is our future is necessarily limited by the past. Only insofar as we are attached to the past do we remain bound to a pattern of karma, which is simply the inertia of our previous actions.

To be attached to the past is to inevitably repeat it, to structure our life according to its fixed patterns. To be attached to the past is to be bound to an identity, a personal becoming through time. It is to fall into the stream of tendencies and impressions of the entire material evolution developed over time and history. This places us under the influence not only of our individual karmic latencies but also those of the collective mind. It opens the door to the dark forces of what was and what should be no more.

Through memory we come under the power of mortality because the past is inherently devoid of true life, duration and creativity. We only gain the repetitive continuity of a material thing, not the dynamic creativity of a conscious subject. To be attached to the past is to be identified with the external, because only the external can leave a mark in time. The internal, the *state of seeing* that is our awakened consciousness, is the presence that cannot pass away. Karma is the inertia of matter that we become bound to when we identify ourselves with the body and mind and fall under their domination.

We fall under the influence of karma when we seek our fulfillment in the domain of time, which is the past moving into the future. Our lack of awareness in the present binds us to a destiny. What particular karmic pattern we fall into is not the real issue, however pressing it may be. All karma is an ignorance of the present that binds us to the limited pattern of the past, and subjects us to the fluctuations of time as joy and sorrow, pleasure and pain, birth and death. The details of our karma are not important but, rather, why we allow ourselves to fall under the influence of the external world in the first place.

> **Our lack of awareness in the present binds us to a destiny.**

As conscious subjects, we have no karma, which only belongs to an object. Only when we throw away the integrity of our awareness to become somebody or something in the material world do we come under the forces of time. When we cease to define ourselves in terms of action, which is karma, we will discover that we have no duties and no obligations. This does not mean that we cannot act, but that our action will be free of desire and external seeking, and therefore an expression of liberation. Such action free of time has the capacity to bring about transformation on all levels, individually and collectively.

The Knowledge
and the Ignorance

T wo primary forces work within the universe—the Knowledge and the Ignorance *(Vidya* and *Avidya).* Ignorance works through our subconscious compulsions, dispersing the light of knowledge into the external world, where we lose our true being. This ignorance is based on a belief in an external reality, a bodily identity and a self that is separate from other selves. It is not simply personal but a cosmic force creating materiality, density and inertia.

Knowledge is the inner light that reveals the self-sufficient reality of being. We all sense this deeper knowledge in our intrinsic yearning for the eternal, the pure and the real. This higher knowledge is self-knowledge, which is not personal identity, but the perception of the entire universe within our own hearts. It is a cosmic force of awareness, freedom and creativity.

We must learn to move from the Ignorance to the Knowledge, which, to use an ancient Vedic prayer, is to cross over from non-being to being, from darkness to light, from death to immortality. This is the path of discrimination, which takes us beyond illusion to truth. Our false identity or separate self is discarded. Our eternal nature or true Self is revealed, like the sun that shines forth after an eclipse.

To find the truth we must negate the falsehood that obscures it, which is the main method of the yogic path of knowledge. However, this is not to leave us in a state of negativity but to remove the veils so that our inner light, which is self-effulgent, perfectly pure and full, will no longer be obscured.

Limitation and the Unlimited

L ife presents us with both the limited and the unlimited. On one hand, there is no limit to what we can see or experience. On the other hand, there is a definite limit to what we can do and the time that we have to live.

If we examine any object in nature we will discover that there is no end to the details of its appearance. Take a walk in the woods and try to see everything around you. Examine the endless detail on a rock, the bark of a tree, the many insects, the pattern of the dew or the movement of the clouds. The unlimited is everywhere. Yet we also find specific limits to things. Each thing has restrictions as to its size and duration. The world presents us with both the limited and the unlimited. How do these factors relate? Which is primary or real? Have we ever examined this issue, or have we merely accepted the limited as the real?

If we pursue the limited we will find it everywhere. We will find boundaries to everything. If we pursue the unlimited we will also find it everywhere. We will find no end to the beauty, uniqueness and variety of life. If we pursue the limited we ourselves will become limited, trapped in time and matter. If we pursue the unlimited we ourselves will become unlimited. We will open into the eternal and the infinite.

Unfortunately, in our society we emphasize the limited side of life. We establish territories, distinctions and definitions. We price and label things and people and lose contact with the indescribable richness of perception. Rather than possess the entire universe in consciousness, we hold to a few paltry items on the physical plane, which itself is vicarious. We miss the unlimited and so never find lasting peace.

The world is the unlimited under apparent limitation. If we look superficially we see the limited. If we look deeply we perceive the unlimited. The unlimited abides in the state of seeing, our own awakened consciousness, not in any object seen. Thought focuses on the limited and pronounces it to be real. In this way we limit our own reality. Awareness reveals the unlimited, not as a theory but as the fact of perception. Which of these two directions in consciousness we choose determines our own reality, and our happiness or sorrow.

Memory—
A Burden We Cling To

T he real possessions that bind us are our memories, our inner possessions. Memory is an attachment, a holding on to an experience, an accumulation in which energy is trapped. Memory is a form of matter, a substance in the mind. It is the residue of an experience that has left a mark within us. The degree of our attachment to the past, to a personal history, is the degree of our materialism. Our memories form the landscape of the world of illusion and sorrow, Samsara, in which we are caught.

This world of memory is revealed during dream and fantasy. It underlies our waking consciousness and distorts our perception. Hence our fall into dream or fantasy is a fall into the inertia of our own minds. The more we are attached to the past and to a personal becoming in time, the heavier is the weight of our ignorance. That is why as we grow older our life becomes more weary, more of a burden. It holds more memory that pulls us downward.

We can easily measure our spiritual ignorance in life: it is equal to the density of our thoughts, our habitual stream of memory-based considerations. Similarly, the knowledge that we cling to through thought is the measure of the matter in our minds that obstructs us from seeing the truth.

We are not bound to the external world or to the matter outside of us. It is the world inside us, the matter within our own minds that binds us. Only when we take the world inside ourselves through thought does it become a burden and cause worry and anxiety. If we let the world be, it takes care of itself in the natural harmony and freedom of existence.

Consciousness is immaterial and thought is matter. To fall into thought is to introduce a foreign substance (matter) into our unbounded consciousness and to weigh it down. Our thoughts are our matter, through which we fall into the material world and its compulsions. To acquire things mentally through name, recognition and identification is to add to the ignorance within us.

> **The mind empties itself naturally.**

The mind empties itself naturally—consciousness itself is emptiness, immateriality and boundless space—when we do not fill it with cares and anxieties. The realization that thought is a burden is the ending of thought. All worry and care is a useless weight that separates us from the beneficence of existence, drawing upon us the very disharmonies that we wish to avoid. When we release the burden of thought through the perception of its foreign nature, we transcend the entire world.

Opposition and Understanding

O) pposition is not the way of understanding. It does not resolve our problems but only intensifies them. Opposition is the very way of conflict, through which conflict must increase. Why do we oppose things and what kind of consciousness does opposition breed?

The opposer is the opposed and both are opposition, which is resistance, duality and conflict. We try to arrive at security in the outer world by overcoming our opposition, the enemy. Yet this creation of the enemy destroys security and puts us ever on guard. We can only solve our problems when we face them together as the common human problem, not when we see the other as the problem. To see others as the enemy denies the unity of humanity through which alone humane action is possible. As people become negative value for us, so we become negative value for them, which posits our own denigration and destruction.

We use this same mentality of opposition to approach our inner problems. To get rid of anger we oppose it, struggle against it and try to end its existence. We treat it as the enemy, an alien force to be defeated. We end up becoming angry with our anger, as the effort to end anger only creates more anger. The same scenario occurs with desire, fear or whatever psychological state we try to change. Our effort to change it only perpetuates it.

Opposition is the way of matter, which is built up by dualistic forces of elemental attraction and repulsion. Hence opposition renders us more materialistic, dull and insensitive. Opposition is the way of division. To see something as other, as contrary, is to divide our own consciousness, to split up reality and create fragmentation.

We cannot end the existence of anything. The existence of all things is eternal and sacred. Negative emotions exist because we do not live with reverence. Feelings of opposition only come to an end when we treat them with reverence, when we liberate the energy caught within them by not seeing them as other than ourselves.

For this reason yogic teachings symbolize emotions, including negative emotions like anger or fear, in the form of various Gods and Goddesses, including wrathful deities. Our emotions are truly Gods and Goddesses. They are great powers of the collective psyche—cosmic forces—and not personal possessions that we can control. To approach them with reverence affords them the space of transformation. This does not mean to fall under their influence but to be receptive to the truth that they convey. Negative emotions teach us that the consequence of all personal seeking is suffering.

Whatever we approach with unity can be resolved. Whatever we approach with duality only causes further conflict. In the unity of the perceiver and the perceived, all things become doors to the sacred, even suffering and death.

Perception and Preconception

T he mind is not an objective or detached intelligence. It possesses a hidden motive, which is to maintain its conditioning. The mind acts based upon an assumption that it tries to impose upon reality. It is not open but comes with a point of view that it seeks to justify. Therefore, the mind is never really capable of impartial judgement.

The mind cannot be free of preconception because the mind is a preconception. The mind cannot be free of prejudice (prejudgement) because it is a formation of prejudice. Prejudice and preconception are fully dissolved only when thought is put to rest. Thought always functions from a center, a point of view that posits an ego. Its knowledge is aimed at modifying reality to protect this central fixation, which is the blind spot it cannot really question.

Life has an infinite abundance of phenomena and many layers of reality. It is possible to find justification for almost any point of view and to arrive at a rationality in which almost anything can appear incontrovertible. The commercial man judges everything in terms of monetary value, the scientist in terms of calculable forces, and so on. Each view has plenty of data to work with, but fails to perceive the whole of life that lies outside its bias.

We question life in terms of our preconceptions, and the mind naturally tends to uphold them. This is not because life justifies our preconceptions but because we reflect them onto life. That is why, though there are innumerable points of view, each person tends to comfortably think that he or she or their group alone is truly right.

All mental theories and deductions from facts are limited and ultimately false. They are tied to a center and its boundaries. Whatever thought does must remain naïve, egocentric, and of only superficial or temporary value. It is not an issue of needing better information but of dissolving that center for direct perception to occur.

It is a mistake to see life in terms of a particular thing or idea, whatever our assumption may be. To really see life, we must observe things as they are. Ordinarily we project our thoughts upon life, trying to make it fit into their narrow groove. And if life does not fit the pattern of our thoughts—and eventually it will not—then we reject life, which only brings about decay or death.

> **To find truth we must be motiveless.**

The mind's central fixation is its substratum, and to remove it would dissolve the mind itself. As with all things, the mind has an inherent desire to continue its existence, however painful it may be. Therefore, freeing the mind from prejudice means freeing ourselves from the mind.

We are caught in motivations and manipulations that make us miss the beauty and fulfillment that are intrinsic to being aware. Our preconceptions destroy perception, which only occurs when the mind is open and free of attachment. Our motivations destroy right action, which only occurs spontaneously as the response of true intelligence to the present. To find truth we must be motiveless. This is to be one with the universal motive, which is to bring a higher consciousness into the world.

Presence and
the Present Moment

$\left(\text{Y}\right)$ ogic teachings emphasize awareness in the here and now, or being in the present moment. This has often been misunderstood. For most of us, being in the present means getting into what is happening around us. It implies experiencing the moment and its immediate pleasure and pain, which is the pursuit of sensation. This is to become driven by the stream of events like a leaf by the wind. To be such a creature of the present moment is to have no enduring values in life.

The true present is not of time. The present that lies between the past and the future is an insubstantial moment that has no reality of its own. It is the most fleeting and insignificant of things. The true present is the presence of consciousness which observes time but does not change along with it. In that presence the images of time appear like bubbles or clouds that can have no real substance.

The way to truth is not to try to hold on to the present moment, which does not endure even for an instant, but to remain in the eternal presence of consciousness. The true presence has no form or motion, though it is reflected in all things. To open up to that presence is to no longer be disturbed by the transient events around us, but to embrace all time as the process of perception.

True meditation requires not dwelling in the present moment, but dwelling in presence. Presence is Being, which is in all things, in all time and beyond.

Reality and Appearance

A ppearance is never reality and reality never appears. They are two different dimensions altogether. Whatever appears is bound by duality and relativity, whereas reality is only one and absolute.

This is not a statement of abstract philosophy. Neither our reality nor that of the world can be found in the realm of appearances as revealed by the senses, or by any extension of sensory knowledge including the subtlest scientific instruments. Reality is the inner consciousness that can never become an object of examination for the externally oriented mind. Similarly, whatever we can observe or see must be ultimately unreal because it is not the awareness within.

The world and how we appear within it can never be the truth. We will never find reality in the world of appearances, just as a light cannot be found by tracing its shadows on the wall. Appearance is name, form and limitation, which remain trapped in alternating waves of pleasure and pain, joy and sorrow, birth and death. Appearance can never become perfect. It remains relative, bound by duality, shifting up and down but never arriving at any lasting state.

Whatever world we appear to be in, and whatever body we appear to inhabit, is never real. They are reflections of our inner consciousness, like the waves that rise from the sea. They are products of an outgoing view based upon thought in ignorance of our true Self.

We cannot find peace or fulfillment in any appearance, however great. Only in the d of consciousness does our innate happiness abide. This is not to denigrate the outer world but simply to see it as it is. The world of appearance is like an image, symbol or play—a magic show lasting a few days. It has its wonder and beauty but it does not have any reality of its own. To believe that any appearance is real is to be taken in by appearances. To see the illusory nature of all appearances is to allow reality to shine forth, through which we pass beyond all illusions.

Relationship and the Self

We are not only related to everything that we see, we *are* everything that we see. The sense of Self is universal, not the property of any particular creature or species. The same Self-sense through which we feel ourselves to exist can be found in all creatures. That Self-awareness unites us all.

In the pursuit of relationship we are really seeking to discover ourselves beyond the boundaries of the physical body. The other is but a reflection of our Self into the external world. The entire universe is a manifestation of our own deeper being. In our being we are naturally one with all. Through relationship we are trying to rediscover that unity. Yet that unity can never be gained on a mere physical level, in which we are divided into separate bodies. It is only possible in consciousness that is not limited by time and space.

Real relationship is to see ourselves in all beings and all beings within ourselves. The Self is present not only in human beings, but in plants and animals as well. It dwells in the rivers, mountains, clouds and stars. There is a consciousness in the wind, the fire and the rain. The Sun and Moon are also living beings. The Spirit is everywhere in nature. The Divine person sees with all eyes and moves with all feet. Once we realize this we can never feel isolated or alienated. We will find communion everywhere, even in silence and solitude.

Contacting the true Self is the ending of all sorrow, loneliness and separation. It is discovering real relationship, which is to being one with all. If we are open to that Self in all beings, the world will be one family and beat with one heart.

Renunciation

T rue renunciation does not mean giving up something, like setting aside material things in order to gain something spiritual. Renunciation means not taking things up in the first place, not trying to find happiness through a pattern of mental or material accumulation. To do this we must be in harmony with the movement of life that clings to nothing. Renunciation is not an intended action of giving something up, but the freeing of the mind from ulterior motives. There is nothing that we have to give up other than our own need to control things.

True renunciation is natural and easy, the casting off of all stress and tension in openness to life's natural beneficence. It is the realization that there is nothing to lose, and that what is truly ours must come to us of its own accord if we do not obstruct it. Trying to force things may have some result but it will be artificial. It will have to be maintained by force and in the end will revert to its original state.

Whatever we try to give up or renounce we are really picking up. We are still attached to the idea that we can control things. We remain bound by the thought of the thing, and it makes little difference whether that thought is positive or negative.

As long as we think that there is something to renounce we have not renounced anything. For true renunciation to occur, the sense of separate action must be given up, including the idea that we can change ourselves. We try to gain by taking things up or setting them down, but this very effort to acquire and achieve causes us to lose. Whatever we divide ourselves from, either to acquire or to avoid, defeats us because we are dividing a unitary reality into conflicting opposites.

True renunciation is not rejection or avoidance; it is not trying to get rid of anything or to live up to some standard of austerity. It is being open to what is intrinsically ours rather than trying to make something belong to us. All things come to us when we no longer seek them. This is like a man and his shadow. All creation is our shadow that will follow us of its own accord if we do not try to follow after it.

The nature of matter, which the mind shares, is to expand or contract. As long as we are caught in materiality, our main project is to expand or contract. The giving up of this blind intention of matter to expand or contract is the true renunciation, which is incalculable, spontaneous and unmotivated. It is the acceptance of all existence as sacred, in which all sense of gain and loss born of memory dissolves in the beauty and bliss of awareness. Only if we think there is something to gain can we lose. All existence is ever full and overflowing when we set aside the idea of possession. There is nothing to acquire or discard because there are no "things," because matter is a construct of the mind in a conscious universe where all is one.

> **There is nothing that we have to give up other than our own need to control things.**

Security and Insecurity

O ur main worry in life, if we look deeply, is for our welfare in the material world—whether or not we will have enough income to get by, whether our job or relationship will be secure, whether our health will be good, and so on. This problem constantly gnaws at us, keeping us disturbed and disoriented. It may fall into the background, particularly in periods of good fortune, but eventually resurfaces with the various difficulties that life brings to us. To assuage this fear, we look to improve our position in the world: to get a better job, to save more money, to have insurance, property or other material supports.

Yet however much we accumulate, we are never able to conquer this basic fear. Greater income means greater expenses, while more possessions give more to worry about. And there are always obstructions and enmity from one side or another. We gain in one area but lose in another. We may, for example, gain wealth but lose our friends.

Most of us are plotting to expand our position in the world in order to gain more security. We look to friends, family, employers, banks and governments to guarantee our status or to save us if we are poor. We seek our refuge in life in something outside ourselves. Yet no matter how apparently secure a few of us may become, there remain depressions, wars, revolutions and natural calamities to fear along with disease, old age and death, which are our inevitable lot.

Even those of us who are spiritually inclined become easily disturbed by financial, legal, political or health problems. Our personal welfare in the outer world is our prime value. And when this is threatened we feel that our whole life is at risk.

Only if we feel safe materially do we find the leisure for higher pursuits like art or meditation, or we can afford to be charitable.

However, the very outward powers that we rely upon for security are themselves insecure. The government, the insurance companies, our family, whoever we have made our refuge, can become a threat. Our looking to the material world for security places us under the rule of the external. It allows us to become unbalanced by the changes and fluctuations which are the very nature of life. Our seeking of outer security, which does not really exist, breeds insecurity. It makes us dependent upon the external, which is unreliable, and causes us to lose our innate integrity and independence in awareness.

There is no security in the material world. The nature of matter is corruption, dependency and relativity. How can the transient give us support? The pursuit of security is endless because outwardly there is nothing that we can really hold on to. The only outward certainty is death. Yet most of us are not concerned with death. We are worried about how we will get by in old age—whether our family or someone else will take care of us, whether or not we will be sick. We seldom consider the fact of death that nullifies all personal happiness and sorrow.

All life supports the one who is aware. This is the law of life: all beings further the one who feels unity with them. This support is not a dependable income or freedom from tribulation, but the peace and love which transcend death and sorrow. The spiritual life does not depend upon material security but on the unfoldment of self-knowledge. Our true Self does not bow down to those who have power, wealth or prestige. Those who hold the power externally are no more than puppets in a stage show, pulled by strings they do not see.

Sensitivity and Sensation

We have many forms of heightened sensation to pursue in the modern world. Entertainment, travel, romance, new clothes, new equipment or new ideas are all a pursuit of sensation. Even much of the spiritual life is a pursuit of sensation in the form of inner colors, lights, sounds and blissful experiences.

Truth only comes to a mind that is not pursuing sensation, that has the capacity to look within. Sensation is not sensitivity but, rather, breeds insensitivity. The pursuit of sensation leads us to brighter colors, louder music and greater speed. It jades the mind, makes the body heavy and takes us out of harmony with the greater joy of existence. Sensation is a form of materialistic seeking in which we strive to take in more and more pleasurable experiences. To accumulate sensation is to become dense and heavy with matter, which produces boredom and fatigue.

How do we empty the mind of sensation? We must first stop filling our minds with it. This begins when we see the illusion and sorrow that the pursuit of sensation leads to. Sensation must have a negative effect upon the mind, just as junk food causes toxins in the body. Sensation increases artificial appetites and breeds agitated and confused actions.

To end sensation we must stop thinking about our sensory experiences, cease mulling them over in our minds. We must engage in a way of meditation to empty the mind. Only the inquiring mind has the energy not to fall into the allure of sensation.

We must reorient our perception. We should cease looking for sensation and become sensitive to existence, both as the visible and the invisible, both as nature and the Divine. This means that the perception of a cloud is as important as the latest movie. It means that emptiness and silence are as real as any sight, sound or touch.

To empty the mind of sensation does not mean that we have to close our eyes and ears, though turning our attention within is essential. It does not mean to make ourselves insensitive to life. On the contrary, it requires that we are more sensitive to the real nature of things and cease following mere appearances. This sensitivity includes both the realm of the senses and beyond.

There is in all things, including those of the sensory world, the presence of the light of consciousness. To be sensitive to that light is to really see and to really feel.

Suffering and Awakening

I t is not necessarily sad that we suffer, that we experience pain, disease or even death. The real sadness is that we have lost consciousness of our true nature in which there is peace even in the midst of pain, misfortune and iniquity. This loss of true awareness is the real cause of emotional suffering, which in turn makes physical suffering hard to endure. Nor is it necessarily good that we experience happiness, health and longevity. These may only afford us a greater bondage to the outer world if we don't use them for some higher purpose.

Our human creaturely drama is no more real than any other drama or show. Our personal identities are little more than masks. Our joys and sorrows are not different from those of dream creatures. We must see our insignificance and no longer be taken in by appearances. Our joy and sorrow are equally transient and unreal. It is the separate self, caught in its self-projected drama of gain and loss, from which we need release. Our great collective dramas—our wars, revolutions, great social progress or religious revivals—are also not real. Groups, like individuals, come and go in the nature of creation like waves on the sea.

> We should not try to flee suffering but to understand it.

Suffering is an energy to awaken us to truth, to get us to question who we really are. The sad thing is that the sufferings which are inevitable in life do not awaken us to the falseness of our personal seeking.

Matter is inherently suffering because it is the limited. To experience suffering is to face the inherent limitation of material existence. We should not try to flee suffering but to understand it, discover the truth of life that it reflects. Then suffering liberates us into joy.

Only when we allow our suffering to liberate us can we become liberated from suffering. Suffering is the breaking of the boundaries of the known and the familiar. If we are open to the truth of it, suffering cleanses and transforms us.

The Universal Religion

T rue religion is universal and eternal. It is life and truth, existence itself. It is not something that one can join or be excluded from. It cannot be possessed, and those who claim to own it have lost it. The universal religion is the universal consciousness and love. It requires that we live according to the great laws or dharmas of life, the foremost of which is the unity of all beings.

What can be organized or codified is not the spiritual or life, but matter, which is death. Organized religion is the spiritual petrified, made into another formula or slogan. Therefore, to discover true spirituality we must put the divisions of organized religion behind us. We enter into what is truly spiritual only to the extent that we transcend external identifications of class, creed and nationality. This requires that we perceive the oneness of all as a fact of life. The truly religious mind can identify with all things in the oneness with truth. To the extent that we have an exclusive identity we fall from the spiritual—which is everything and nothing—and become a mere label, proponent or propagandist.

All true religious teachings have their heart in the universal truth that is the life beyond the mind, the intelligence that dwells beyond the division of words and thoughts. But this we must discover for ourselves, through our own meditation practice. It requires the patient labor of awareness for which there is no substitute. To the extent, therefore, that we discover the truth of any spiritual teaching, we are no longer limited to its particular names and forms. We are not bound to its indicators—limited as they are by time, place and person—but see the universal truth that stands in itself.

A spiritual teaching only has value to the extent that it does become an end-in-itself, that it does not make ultimate any particularities of time, place and person. Religion in the ordinary sense with its dogmas and beliefs is more a hindrance than a help to the search for truth. The real goal is to enter into our true nature beyond the division of thought and belief. True religion leads us to our true Self, not to any person, book or institution as final.

The Waters of Life

T rue life is not a material thing. It is not an object, energy or idea. It is not physical, emotional or mental. True life is consciousness and awareness where there is no division, for division is death. Consciousness is the ocean of immortal life. Those who are aware have the real power of life. They can give life and make things endure.

The true place of the human being in creation is to bring the waters of immortal life into the garden of the natural world. The true place of the spiritual teacher, the seer, is to bring the waters of life into the garden of human culture. However, owing to the lack of true consciousness in human beings, this garden now resembles a desert in which fierce dust storms blow.

To be is to give life. No action or idea gives life, only being itself. The creative products of the natural or human worlds are the plants that grow from this water of life, which is pure consciousness. These plants do not grow of themselves, however beautiful or significant they may appear to be. They grow from the water, which they draw spontaneously without even recognizing it. For a true culture, there must first of all be the waters of life. All will follow naturally from that, and without it growth will be artificial and self-destructive.

Because we seek results and value productions, we have lost contact with the streams of life. Our work lacks a firm foundation and is incapable of providing real nourishment. Greater effort or efficiency will not suffice. The patience, restraint and quiescence of the essence are required, a silent communion with the depths of the heart. From this arises a creation that is not bound by the past or the future, which is both yesterday and tomorrow.

Wonder and Awe

A ll life is a mystery; this is self-evident. Life can never be explained. Its mysterious nature is its being, fullness and transcendence. If life were explainable it would be nothing, a piece of information, or a set of mathematical formulas.

Explanations are possible only for inert and mechanical things, but where there is life and consciousness, explanations are a violation. Why explain a flower? Its self-evident beauty, which is a mystery beyond all explanation, is enough. In the seeing of life, the seeing which is life, all things are full. They need not be described or defined to have value. We seek explanations because we are not aware of the self-evident mystery. This seeking to define consigns us to the limitations of our own minds.

All existence overflows with abundance and grace that result not from effort but from letting go. All is mystery, grace and giving. There is no one to thank and no need to look back or to try to hold onto anything. One can only respond with wonder, awe and reverence as part of the magic and mystery that is our own existence beyond the boundaries of thought.

> **Life can never be explained.**

Because we seek explanations, which are merely words, our lives have lost their meaning. Only because we have lost contact with the mystery and are no longer open to it do we need to be entertained. Reality is the unknown that dwarfs all that we know. Only what cannot be measured and is inherently a mystery can have real value and be worthy of reverence.

There is no dilemma in the mystery of existence. There is a dilemma only when we seek to explain existence. That is to fall from its plenitude into the narrow groove of thought which is always problematical. Let us dare to be unknown and to be one with existence, which is the unknown. Anything else is not to be a real human being but a formula that can be figured out.

The mystery of life is a self-evident joy. Falling from that joy into the sorrow of separate existence, we must seek something outside because we are empty inside. But emptiness cannot be explained away. Thought as the known is emptiness in which there are only problems or, at best, limited and questionable solutions. What fills the mind is not any idea or emotion, but the mystery that is the energy of consciousness, in which all is direct vision, full in itself and ever free.

PART III

The Practice of Meditation

Yoga is the negation of the thought-composed
mind. Then the seer abides in his own nature.

Patanjali, *Yoga Sutras* I. 2-3

Concentration is connecting the mind to a single place.
Meditation is sustaining a single perception there.
Realization occurs when the mind as if devoid of
itself abides in the truth of the object meditated on.

Patanjali, *Yoga Sutras* III. 1-3

In this section we will examine the practical issues of meditation and its different methods from beginning to advanced levels. We will look at various meditation practices from the standpoint of Self-inquiry and related Vedantic approaches.

The Alchemy of Perception

T here is an eternal alchemy of awareness, an inner process
through which our gross and mortal nature, the ego-mind,
is transmuted into pure consciousness and immortality. This
teaching is hidden in many ancient rituals, symbols and mytholo-
gies involving fire and water as the two basic powers of creation.
The purpose of our existence is not to accumulate things or to
become somebody in the outer world but to give birth to a new
consciousness. This process is not something artificial that occurs
through strain or force. It is part of the natural movement of life,
of which all outer transformations are mere metaphors. For this
inner birth to occur our internal energies must be purified, sub-
limated and balanced in the right manner.

Two factors are present in all that we perceive: the seer and
the seen, which are the conscious subject and the material or
formed object. The true seer is the state of seeing itself. It is not
the entity created by thought but the inner Self or awareness of
transcendence that endures behind all the fluctuations of our
apparent identity. The seen is whatever this consciousness illumines, the movements of the mind and senses which include all
that we know as the outer world.

All that we know dwells within the field of seeing and, as the
manifestation of that field, is seeing itself. Everything, behind its
appearance, conceals an essence that gives energy to consciousness. Each thing speaks to us and reveals some truth of life
and reality. When the light of seeing illumines the object that
we see, then the essence of the object comes forth as bliss.

Perception distills the essence of reality, but for this to occur
our perception must be pure. It must be direct and unmediated

by any conditioned idea or belief, unclouded by any thought or intention, beyond any judgement of good and bad, and free of any choice as to what we want to see. True perception is not of time or of the mind. It reveals nothing that can be conceptually known, but the energy of immortality—the substance of the eternal that is the ground of existence.

For this alchemy to work within us we must change the direction of our attention. We must give reverence to all that we see rather than merely use it to gain some personal goal. We must make our minds into the crucible and the matrix for the coming into being of the unknown. Our daily lives must become an offering and a prayer not limited to any name or form. Then for us to see will be to be, and to be all and everlasting.

Channeling and Meditation

$\left(C \right)$ hanneling is not a new phenomenon. It is another way of opening the mind to the subtle or astral plane, which is much vaster than the physical realm that we ordinarily are limited to. Such an interest in mediums, trances and seances is as old as the human race. While realms subtler than the physical can afford us greater knowledge or power, they still fall short of the reality that transcends all appearances.

To perceive the ultimate truth we must silence the mind through meditation. For meditation to be effective we must develop the power of attention and not give our awareness away to some other force, even if it appears to be of a higher nature. Meditation is not a trance in which some other entity speaks through us, but a heightened state of self-awareness in which we are conscious of our own eternal nature.

Actually we are always channeling because nothing really belongs to us, nor is any identity that we assume really our own. Our thoughts and feelings, even our sense of self, come from outside our true nature which is pure consciousness alone. Such channeling only comes to an end when we dissolve the ego, which keeps us dependent upon an external source for our reality. Yet to stop channeling some person, entity or ego, we must channel the truth. This is to turn the mind into a vessel for consciousness. Such a mind does not see name and form, self or other, this world or another, but only the sacred.

> **To perceive the ultimate truth we must silence the mind through meditation.**

While inwardly we should seek to connect ourselves with the Divine and with spiritually realized teachers, we must be careful about opening ourselves to the influences of the astral plane.

Subtle matter contains a subtle ego that has much allure for the mind that is not trained in meditation. This does not mean there is anything wrong with exploring the astral plane that holds the occult forces of life. We should, however, not confuse exploring a subtler realm of manifestation with the search for truth that is beyond all worlds.

Channeling is often a substitute for a guru or for direct contact with the guiding force of consciousness, for which there can be no real substitute. If we seek such direct guidance, by making ourselves receptive to it, we will find it. But if we content ourselves with indirect guidance we may fall into further illusions. We should not confuse channeling, which is at best a way to access subtle knowledge, with meditation, which is the sovereign way to go beyond thought and its sorrow.

Concentration and
How to Develop It

T o transcend the mind and its many thoughts we must be able to hold consistently to a single thought. We must have the power to fully apply our attention in a single direction without distraction. In our ordinary undeveloped state, our thoughts are fragmented and move in various ways that lose the energy of attention. Such a scattered mind can never arrive at any real understanding. First we must learn to concentrate, to sustain our minds on a particular inquiry. This requires that we have a real interest in finding the truth. It cannot be done as a mere curiosity or diversion.

Attention is like the muscle that must be developed by degrees. One can start by focusing on simple external objects like a candle flame or something attractive in the world of nature like the sky, a mountain or a tree. Then we can proceed to internal objects, visualizing the form of a God, Goddess or teacher that communicates some higher reality to us. From internal images we can move to concentration on a mantra or abstract geometrical forms like yantras or mandalas. This eventually provides us with the ability to focus on deep inquiries like the question "Who am I?", which is the real goal. If we have little concentration to begin with, we must develop it slowly and consistently, in a step-by-step manner. Once we have mastery of concentration, by its power we can uncover all the secrets of the mind.

Unfortunately, we are conditioned to carelessly give our attention away. This is most of what we call entertainment, in which we give our awareness to another person or to some medium. We get fascinated with external personalities and dramas, failing to see that we are no longer in control of our own thoughts. Whatever we lose our attention to cannot raise us up in life but only makes us more asleep to the truth.

Without one first possessing the power of concentration, meditation easily becomes an exercise in false imagination. When we try to meditate we get lost in our unfocused thought current and its habits. To move through the mind, just as to travel on the sea, we need the proper vehicle. Concentration is the boat that allows us to cross the confused sea of the unconscious.

If we wish to really meditate we must first learn the art of concentration and become capable of directing our attention at will. Yet to be able to concentrate is not easy, and like any exercise requires initial work and struggle. We may prefer to simply meditate naturally, but without concentration this may be wandering in our own distracted thoughts.

Conscious Will

(M) any of us see the need for Self-realization, yet we are unable to go far along the way of its practical attainment. We find it extremely difficult to change ourselves, particularly our old attachments. We simply lack the will power to be consistent in our efforts. Our will has no focus. We decide to do one thing, but soon afterwards another idea or desire intrudes into our minds and we go off in a disparate direction.

Most of us have no real conscious will in life. We have habits, compulsions and addictions, but we are seldom able to hold to any project consistently and energetically. Our very thought process, which runs automatically after external things, is the destruction of will, which depends upon detachment. Becoming, our search for identity in time, is the ending of will, which is being. Assertion, the attempt to project the self, is the negation of will, which is surrender.

Will is developed by the power of attention. It can only be gained to the extent that we do not give ourselves over to entertainment and self-indulgence. Desire fragments the will and scatters it into the outer world. True will relinquishes desire, recognizing that desire arises from an external compulsion rather than from an internal creativity.

Will is developed by the power of attention.

Without will we cannot go far on the spiritual path. Yet will is not gained by conflict or struggle, only through patience and perseverance. Will comes through presence, not through the desire to achieve, which, positing a result, fragments our energy into time. True will is surrendering to *what is,* merging into the energy of existence. This is the greatest achievement, but it also requires the greatest sacrifice, the surrender of personal seeking.

To regain our true will in life we must stand above desire and not take its fantasies as our own. The problem is that we confuse will with desire. We think that will is getting what we want. But desire comes from the external world and binds us to various objects within it. The will to get what we want is not true will at all, only heightened desire. To be able to get what we want creates further craving, in which we become more weak and addicted.

True will is freedom from desire. It is the capacity to endure the vicissitudes of life, to remain at peace in gain and loss, joy and sorrow, pleasure and pain. Otherwise we are slaves to the outer world, regardless of whatever we may own or accomplish.

The Creative State

T hought itself is not creative, though the creative can manifest through the mind and its actions. The basis of thought is karma, which is reaction, the continuation of the past according to a lack of awareness in the present. Therefore, we cannot become creative merely through thought. We may fabricate all kinds of things through the thought-based mind, but they will remain artificial, shadows of what used to be.

To become creative in consciousness, rather than in some particular field, requires going beyond the patterns of thought and memory. This means not accepting the false creativity of thought as legitimate. We must cease to throw our creativity outside ourselves in the pursuit of sensation and information. Creativity arises naturally when we are sensitive to life that no thought can limit. This is not a matter of technique or effort, but the natural capacity and power of attention.

True creativity is found not in the effort to be creative or in the cultivation of talent. Talent itself is not creative but a form of training, a special conditioning arrived at through thought. True creativity does not display itself or seek recognition. It may not even express itself at all. It reveals itself in silence and emptiness. It finds itself in all existence and does not rest upon a product.

To live in the creative state alone brings transformation. The creative state is consciousness that is one with being itself. Any product that arises from that state is secondary and cannot substitute for its beauty or its power. Awareness is itself the highest form of creativity where there is no thought. The entire universe, all creation resides in it.

The surrender of thought opens the floodgates of creative reality, which takes us to the origin of time and space and beyond. We need not seek to be creative, but only cease clinging to our identity in the past, which is the denial of real transformation. This opens up a higher vision through which new worlds can come into being.

Devotion and Meditation

$\left(\text{T}\right)$ he mind is like the wick of an oil lamp, knowledge is like the flame, but devotion is the oil. Without the fuel of devotion meditation becomes dry, negative and lacking in joy. Therefore, if we wish to truly meditate, we must develop the necessary devotion to support it. But what is true devotion?

True devotion is not mere blind worshipping of a God or guru. It is recognizing that the light of awareness in our hearts is also the light of Divine love. Consciousness itself is caring, compassion and concern. It nurtures and provides for all beings like a great Mother.

Most of our psychological problems arise from a lack of devotion. They exist because we are seeking to be loved rather than willing to give love. Through the cultivation of devotion or love of God we learn to give love to all beings. We emulate a higher Divine source of love and let it flow through us, not only for our own benefit but for the good of all.

A person with devotion cannot ever feel really lonely. Devotion puts us in contact with the Divine presence everywhere, providing a feeling of companionship even with the rocks and the sky. It takes us out of the narrow grooves of the mind and the separative compulsions of the ego, placing us beyond ourselves in the greater universe of consciousness. The true devotee sees the Divine beloved everywhere and is at peace with the entire world.

> **A person with devotion cannot ever feel really lonely.**

Classical Yoga teaches that devotion is the fastest means of gaining Self-realization. But such devotion is not mere thought or emotion. It is the very movement of the heart of awareness as it awakens within us. Love is the natural state of union which is yoga.

Discrimination Between Subject and Object

W e are all conscious of ourselves as subjects. This is what it is to be an individual, a perceiver. We revolt against being treated as an object, being used, and yet this is exactly what we are attempting to do most of the time. We treat others as objects for our pleasure, material gain or social prestige. We use people to get what we want, though perhaps with a certain guilt or by granting them favors along the way. And, even more strangely, we view ourselves as objects, allowing ourselves to be used by others if it furthers our aims.

We have an image of our self as an object in the world. This self-image is how others see us, as if we were no more than an object. We live in this subject-object contradiction. On one hand, we find our value and dignity in being treated like a conscious subject, which is generally what we mean when we ask to be treated like a human being. On the other hand, we seek fulfillment through the attainment of prestige and status, through becoming successful objects in the world.

All unethical actions spring from this treatment of people as mere objects. We cannot manipulate or abuse another person if we see him or her as a human being or conscious subject. It is only possible when we view people as objects, as a means of getting what we want as if ours were the only legitimate subjectivity in the world.

Yet to become an object is inherently painful because it puts us under the limitation of name, image and identity. It places us under the power of others and causes us to take various roles that are never authentic. It turns us into a commodity for consumption and makes our behavior dishonest, motivated and calculated. As a conscious subject, we cannot find fulfillment as a social image or a material commodity. Even if we are successful outwardly, inwardly we will feel empty, having used others and allowed ourselves to be used. When our moment of glory has passed, we will suffer the pain of having been.

There is no fulfillment in achieving any social image, status or prestige. It is to condemn ourselves to domination by the external, to fall into time and end up as a thing of the past. True fulfillment is found only in being a conscious subject. Consciousness is existence, which is the real present. To abide in consciousness, in the state of seeing rather than in an object seen, is to abide in the state of renewal that is the origin of life. Whatever social role we choose is not the true Self, which is free of all images, pretensions and strivings.

The true Self is beyond the duality of subject and object. To discover this we must see all beings as subjects, perceiving the unity of consciousness that is everywhere. It is not to see an "other," but to see the other as oneself. The sense of objectivity, of the "other," causes alienation, conflict and sorrow. Only when the appearance of an object or an other is perceived to be an illusion can we find peace and happiness. Then the world merges within us and all life unfolds itself as an expression of the heart.

Ego, Breath and Sound

(T) he ego is not a conscious intelligence but a subconscious reaction mechanism rooted in the field of nature. Our ego responses of like and dislike, fear and desire, love and hate arise automatically, often contrary to our conscious mind and its social values. That is why ego reactions can be so childish or embarrassing. Our assertive or defensive ego modes, promoting the me and the mine, are often a cause of regret upon later reflection in which we look at our situation objectively, according to the common good.

The ego occurs at a subliminal level, beneath the conscious mind and its discriminating intelligence. It is a vital reaction much like the urges to eat and to breathe. The ego first arose in nature as an instinct of self-preservation, to protect the bodily life. It promotes further animal evolution by heightening the sense of competition and the drive for domination.

The ego therefore is closely connected with the breath and the life-force *(prana)*. It is our personal instinct to greater life, success and achievement. The ego is also closely involved with speech, which occurs through the outgoing breath and represents the expressive power of the vital force.

Controlling the ego is very difficult because the ego occurs automatically, before our reflective powers can manifest. However, through control of the breath or *pranayama,* we can get a handle on it. Through control of speech—through silence, mantra and conscious speech—we can sublimate the ego's manifestation.

The point is not to suppress the ego but to draw our sense of Self to the truly supreme, the Divine Self that is one with all.

This requires feeling the cosmic life and the Divine word, the Divine I-am which absorbs the human I-am into a greater harmony and wholeness.

This Divine I-am, called *aham* in Sanskrit, is inhalation (ah) and exhalation (ha). It is the first of all letters (a) and the last of all letters (h). We all want to be the greatest and cannot stop short of that accomplishment, but this is only possible in God, not in our separate self. If we fully energize our breath, speech and mind in seeking the Divine Self within our hearts, we will be able to attain what is the highest and best for all.

Energizing the State of Seeing

(A) t every moment we can allow our attention to wander in habitual thought patterns, or we can direct it consciously through the cultivation of perception. Usually we are either engrossed in our own mental activities or caught up in sensation. Our mind is not in a truly observant or attentive state.

To develop our attention we must continually reorient the mind to the state of seeing. This can be done in several simple ways. One method is to bring the mind back to the present moment, to engage it in being conscious of *what is,* whether observing ourselves, other people or the natural world.

We can choose any number of objects to develop the power of attention. We can focus on a mantra, on our breathing process, or on an object in the natural world. What is important is not thinking about the object itself but dwelling on its being beyond its particular name and form. What we cultivate in this way is not knowledge about anything in particular but the energy of seeing. Whatever comes to our attention, whether through the senses or through the mind, can be a point of reference back to the presence of consciousness. In this way all that we do functions as a means of promoting awareness.

The most natural point of attention is the inquiry "Who am I?". Whatever we do the thought of the self must arise. We can use this thought in a positive way to inquire into our true nature in being, as opposed to how we identify ourselves in the world of becoming. However, to reach the point of this deep inquiry requires a power of attention that few of us possess. Hence we should begin energizing our state of seeing in our daily lives. Unless we take time to cultivate the state of seeing, we cannot hope to find truth in our lives. Our state of seeing should be our guide and our goal, in which the objects around us become mirrors of our own minds.

The Flame of Awareness

$\left(T\right)$ he quality of our attention is our guiding force in life. We feed it with the thoughts, feelings and impressions that we open ourselves up to on a regular basis. Whatever we do is an offering of our attention to some object or quality that either brings us greater awakening or puts us further to sleep. According to the nature of the object of our attention, our consciousness either grows or withers. Whatever we most give our attention to in our daily lives shows the movement of our mind towards either transformation or decay.

Awareness, like a flame, reveals the essence of truth. How we cultivate this sacred flame determines who we are and what we will become. Most of the time we do not regard our awareness as sacred. We flee the acuteness of its light. We feed it with impure and unclear emotions and thoughts. We strive to put it out. We do not cherish or protect it but waste it away on whatever provides pleasure, self-importance or mere distraction. We must treat our awareness as sacred. Nothing else in life is as meaningful or enduring. Nothing else is as intrinsically our own.

This flame is the Divine Child within us, the offspring of our aspiration and creative work. It is the pure residue of all that we wish to be; the core feeling of the heart that generates oneness and compassion. This Divine Child is born of the Divine Mother, who is the receptive mind—the mind free of thought, choice and ulterior motive, beyond the taint of the separate self. Without first cultivating the field of the receptive mind, which involves being passively aware like the light of the moon, we cannot generate anything that is true and authentic.

This flame takes us to the Divine Father, which is Being itself beyond name and form—the infinite and the eternal that shines like the sun. The transformation of the flame of our attention into the sun of awareness is the process of enlightenment. It takes us beyond birth and death to a continual coming into being of the new that is ever one with the eternal. To bring this about we must be very patient, subtle and silent. It is not arrived at by any dramatic action but by dwelling in emptiness, time-lessness and peace.

> **This flame is the Divine Child within us.**

The Fundamental Question

T here is only one fundamental question in life: "Who am I?". Without knowing ourselves, nothing has validity and our thoughts must breed illusion. In the inquiry into our real nature lies the whole meaning of existence. All else is preliminary or superfluous.

Most of the questions that we ask in life are illegitimate questions because they are based on the assumption that we already know who we are. All our outer knowledge and action is based on the idea that we are who we think we are. If we understand that our self-image is a misconception, what would we feel confident in doing? A man stricken with amnesia will first find out who he is before he tries to figure out who other people are.

This is the colossal ignorance of our entire culture. The entity upon which all our actions are based, the self, is the least critically examined. We have accepted as our true self what other people have told us, what it is customary or stylish to be, or whatever our momentary thought patterns may happen to project. We have molded our identity by external influences, and we cherish this fabricated entity as our real being, seeking to make it happy at all costs.

All of our thoughts are based upon the thought "I": "I am this" or "This is mine," "I need to do this" or "Tomorrow I will do that." The "I" is constantly associated with an object or action, given a name and form, and a becoming in time. The "I" is mixed with an object, an outer identity or self-image. But the "I" in itself is not known to us and never directly approached.

Our knowledge of who we are is indirect and mixed. It is not self-knowledge but self-illusion. We have imposed various outward roles and functions upon our inner self and subjectivity. What we call our self is thus nothing but a series of appearances or pretenses. It is a being for others, not a manifestation of who we really are in our own nature. As long as we project some object or quality upon ourselves, we are projecting our identity into the realm of illusion and materiality. We lose our self and become a thing, which must result in sorrow.

The biggest block to self-knowledge is the idea that we already know who we really are. All that we think we are is merely what we have experienced, the burden of our conditioning. It does not indicate the nature of our consciousness, only the degree of our identification with the external world. Only when we realize the danger of living in that ignorance can we gain the will to progress along the path of truth.

How We Search
for Enlightenment

W) hat we call the mind, the consciousness formed by thought, is material. It is part of the outer world and ruled by its mechanism. Therefore, whatever we do from the standpoint of the mind is materialism, even the search for enlightenment.

In the Vedantic view, to discover what is truly spiritual, one must go beyond the mind and its conditioning. We must dissolve our thoughts down to a subconscious level. This requires profound meditation to calm the mind like a deep lake to reflect the light of truth.

The spiritual cannot arise through any extension of the mind but only through its surrender to the light of "seeing" within. The real search for enlightenment, therefore, has nothing to do with the mind's desire for information and experience. These feed the mind and perpetuate our attachment to the material world and the personal self.

The spiritual work, which is meditation, is the arduous labor of freeing ourselves from the reactions of the mind. It requires actually draining the marshland of the unconscious and its habits and addictions. For this we must see our impulses for what they are—a compulsion of matter that we succumb to through lack of attention. To use the language of ancient mythology, meditation requires that we slay the dragon, the destructive energy of our thought processes arising from spiritual ignorance.

The direct way to discover what is truly spiritual is to move beyond the mind, which is a mechanism of matter. This means recognizing that the mind is not a true intelligence but a subconscious process that we fall into when we fail life's challenge to be aware. The mind is our bondage to the past, which is matter, time and death. It cannot give freedom but keeps us in a limited circle of fear, desire and uncertainty.

Apart from thought there is no entity that is the mind. The mind is a bundle of thoughts, which are confused and in conflict with each other. When the mind is no longer fed with distracted thought, it naturally comes to rest. All of our problems, both individual and collective, come to an end, as our thought stream merges into the ocean of consciousness.

Kundalini, the Power
of Consciousness

T he highest energy belongs to consciousness itself. Consciousness contains the power that has created this entire universe and yet is no way limited or diminished by it.

Where there is awareness, energy follows in its appropriate place. Therefore, if we wish to have more energy, we need only expand the field of our awareness. This is not achieved by having more information about the world but by developing the power of attention.

Kundalini or the "serpent power" is a name given to this energy of consciousness that is transformational in nature. Kundalini is said to dwell asleep at the base of the spine and to unfold the ascending powers of consciousness as it awakens and rises through the *chakras*. While energy follows consciousness, energy can also be used to direct us to consciousness. Stimulating kundalini can help unfold the higher levels of the mind. For this, yogic procedures like mantra and pranayama are employed. Yet such processes must be done with awareness for them to really work. They are meant to assist the process of meditation, which has its own development.

To pursue energy, particularly psychic forces like kundalini, without devotion or inquiry into truth can be dangerous. The subtle energy of the mind is not something to be toyed with or used for purely personal ends. It is not a new sensation, exciting experience or emtional high to be cultivated. Nor can it be developed properly if our emotions are turbulent or if our lifestyle is impure. We must honor the energy of consciousness and make ourselves into the right vessel for it. While certain tools and methods, like breath and mantra, facilitate its unfoldment, they are only gentle aids, not to be used forcefully.

For this reason, kundalini was always revered as a Goddess or Divine power not to be manipulated. Acknowledging it as such ensures its right usage. Kundalini is the energy of the sacred, requiring a respect for the sacred in order to really benefit from it. May that Goddess protect us all and lead us all to our highest potential! We should open to her energy and her will and not simply try to manipulate her power, which is infinite, for our limited ends.

Mantra and the Mind

A long with meditation, the most effective way to decondi-
tion the mind is through the practice of mantra. However,
mantra is both an art and a science that has its right application.
It is not something that can be done mechanically and really
work. Mantra also depends upon the right intention. It must arise
from an aim to develop awareness, not a seeking of personal
power and gain, or it will condition the mind further.

Mantra originally refers to the movement of the mind gener-
ated by the perception of truth. Mantra is the vibration of the
truth that we have perceived. It is the impression on the mind
created by the state of seeing. The perception of truth energizes
our thoughts in a special way, endowing them with focus, clarity and power. This state of the concentrated and attentive mind
is mantra.

Mantra also refers to the repetition of certain sacred sounds,
usually seed-syllables or *bija mantras* like OM or HREEM, which
have a vibratory affinity with the state of seeing. Such primal
sounds are connected to higher levels of consciousness and
energy that contain the keys to all creation. Using such mantras,
or any words of truth and wisdom with deep intent, can reorient the mind to its original state of awareness beyond thought
and the ego.

True mantra is not merely a sound repeated by the conscious
mind, though the practice of the mantra begins at this level. One
must set the mantra in motion within oneself and then listen to
it, allowing it to mirror one's deeper awareness. One then learns
to perceive the mantra as the vibration of truth in all that one
observes.

The mind is composed of distracted thoughts, through which the energy of consciousness is dispersed into the outer world. It is not always possible to bring this confused mass of thought directly to an end. We must develop a unified power of attention in order to control it. This requires keeping our consciousness concentrated on a single point or issue.

Thought is composed of words or sounds, through which we identify ourselves with external objects and qualities. All words and sounds are kinds of mantra or energizations of sound. Mantra is the mind concentrated on a specific sound that has no external meaning in terms of time and space or ordinary reality. Mantra thereby can break our identification with the external world and bring us to our reality in consciousness that is not attached to any form.

The mind possesses a mechanical nature. Mantra works directly on the mechanical mind. It turns the mind's process of calculation and repetition into a means of generating the energy of attention. Mantra is a way of engaging the mechanical mind in the pursuit of truth. Once the mechanical mind is absorbed in the mantra, it loses its attraction to the outer world and can be immersed in concentration and meditation.

> **The mind possesses a mechanical nature.**

How then does one practice mantra? One must continually return the mind to a single thought or mantra, which represents the remembrance of truth or one's own real nature. Any name of the Divine can be used, as such names reflect our connection to our inner consciousness. We should offer the mantra to the Divine or our inner nature, who should be invited to enter into it. We should learn to perceive the mantra as the disclosure of being, the door to silence.

Such mantras must be repeated over a long period of time so that their energy can enter into and change the subconscious mind. It helps to repeat the mantra along with awareness of the breath. The breath itself is unmanifest sound and the basis of all speech. The combination of mantra and pranayama links the mind and vital force and gives more power to each.

One may ask, how can mantra, which is based on thought, be used to negate thought? Thought must be integrated before it can be negated. Mantra integrates thought through the energization of sound and meaning. The attentive mind can then be dissolved through meditation. Hence, until we are in control of our attention, such practices as mantra are indispensable.

The ultimate abode of all mantras is the heart, which is the core of our being from which all thoughts and words arise. The ultimate mantra is the sound of the Self; the *I am all* that is the voice of the spiritual heart manifesting itself as OM.

Pranayama and Meditation

$\left(\text{T}\right)$ he energy of the breath and the energy of thought are directly related. As the breath moves, so does thought. We can observe this for ourselves. When the mind is disturbed, the breath is disturbed; similarly, when the breath is disturbed the mind gets agitated.

By controlling the breath, we can control our thought process down to a subconscious level. By developing the energy of the breath we can increase our energy of concentration and attention. For this reason various breathing practices or styles of pranayama have always been used to facilitate the practice of meditation. Once the breath is calm, it becomes easier to move into the natural state of meditation that depends upon peace of mind.

Our thoughts move outward into the external world by the movement of the breath. Awareness of the breath turns the life-force inward, simultaneously reversing the current of thought. This introverts the mind so that we can observe ourselves with clarity and detachment. The breath is the link between the inner and the outer worlds and can take us in either direction. If we deepen the breath it directs us within. If we let it be agitated it draws us without.

In the process of breathing we not only take in air from the outer world, we also contact the life-force within us, whose ultimate origin is in consciousness. This has great healing and transformative powers. By conscious breathing we can connect with the consciousness behind the breath, allowing us to move beyond the body and mind.

While it is very difficult to get a handle on our thoughts,

which do not abide even for an instant, it is easy to work with the breath. However, to belabor ourselves with our breathing process without inquiring inwardly through meditation is not sufficient. Therefore, combining pranayama with meditation aids in the practice of both.

Pranayama itself can be a form of Self-inquiry. Through the use of the breath we can inquire into the processes of our life and vitality, which underlie the mind. Prana, our internal life-force, has a natural intelligence that transcends the ordinary mind. Through it we can connect with the cosmic intelligence within and around us and bring the beauty and force of all nature into our lives.

> **Pranayama itself can be a form of Self-inquiry.**

Reversing the
Stream of Thought

O rdinarily our thought stream moves outward through the mind and senses into the external world, where it gets us attached to various objects and events in time and space. Meditation consists of turning the thought current around, making it flow back to the fullness of pure consciousness that dwells like an ocean within the heart. This requires that we concentrate and internalize our awareness.

The heart is the ocean of silence where there is no thought, but to reach it we must turn our energy within, which requires deep thinking. This reversal of the thought stream is true inquiry, examining who we are and the truth of our being hidden deep within us. It is also true devotion, seeking the Divine presence at the core of our awareness.

To reverse the thought stream also requires reversing our vital energy, seeking happiness within our own being rather than in external involvements. Our thought stream follows the energy of speech that goes out through the mouth; thus restraining our speech from superficial talk is another aid. The light of awareness goes out through the eyes, so turning our gaze within helps as well.

When all the senses are concentrated within the heart, the mind returns to unity and peace. Our individual awareness becomes part of the Universal Self. This is the real return that we are seeking, the discovery of our true origin in the world within.

Service and Karma Yoga

T he purpose of human life is not to gain personal happiness or to assert our individual rights, though these may have their place. It is to further the evolution of consciousness in the world, which is to work for the good of all. This requires service and self-sacrifice, in which we may have to give up our personal desires for a higher cause.

True service occurs when there is no thought of personal gain, when there is no seeking of reward or recognition for ourselves. It is action done for its own sake, having its own value. If our action is not a form of service it must generate karma or bondage to the external world, and eventually become destructive.

This does not mean that we must engage ourselves in charity or other social and political works, though these can be useful. It means that we should not act out of self-interest but out of surrender to truth. The practice of meditation is the highest form of service in which we offer all mundane and outward activity to the inner power of seeing.

Often the mind is too disturbed or disoriented to meditate, even to chant mantras or do yoga practices. In this case the best way to calm the mind is through work or selfless service. When the body and mind are engaged in work of a service nature, there is no longer the space of distraction for our mind to fall into its own problems.

We only have our personal problems because we are attached to them. If we accept all the world's problems as our own, we will find that our own problems cease to be important and, no longer being fed by our thoughts, naturally dissolve themselves.

We can only become frustrated because we are not seeking to serve but looking to be made happy by others.

Yet even if we are able to meditate easily, the performance of service is very important to integrate that awareness into our daily lives—whether that service is helping others, teaching, writing or simply cleaning the house. As long as our action is self-promoting our meditation cannot be truly effective. Our action becomes meditation when it is not done for personal reward.

The Space Within the Heart

here is a space within ourselves, the space within the heart. It is not a physical space but the space of consciousness itself, the very presence of the Divine. We seldom dwell in this inner space, except in deep sleep, when we return to it unconsciously for rest and renewal.

If we look inside our minds we see emptiness. Most of us fear this emptiness within. We do not like to be alone because we must face this internal emptiness that brings into question our entire existence. We are used to looking and relating externally. We find that to be alone is to be no one, to be unrelated, to have no stimulation and no importance. We flee that inner space and run into outer sensation and involvement. We fill ourselves with the things of the world or occupy ourselves with the things of the mind. This makes our inner space appear frightful. We dread it, as if it were a great suffering or darkness.

But the space within the heart is the most marvelous of all things. The space within the heart contains everything. The entire universe is there, all time and space, and all creation. Past, present and future are there. All our memories, the memories of all things, and all that we could become rest in perfect harmony within it. The fulfillment of all wishes is there. There to see is to be and to be everything and always. All worlds and all creatures dwell in that inner space, woven into a lotus, from the infinitesimal to the infinite. The key to the fulfillment of all wishes is not to pursue them externally but to look for their essence in that space within.

That inner space is full of light like a thousand rising suns. It contains the inner Sun of pure consciousness, of which the outer sun is but a reflection. It holds the inextinguishable flame of our own being, the soul's awareness that persists throughout all our incarnations. In our souls we all dwell around that inner fire like children around their mother, the flame providing nourishment to all. There the original life-force abides that gives vitality and hope to all creatures.

Life dwells in the space within the heart, not merely our personal life, but all life throbbing, pulsating and vibrating everywhere. Our true Self dwells in the space within the heart, ever at peace, far removed from all the worries of the mind and all the strife of the ego. The space within the heart is our true home, in which we can let everything go, including our body and our identity, and become completely free.

This heart space is like a great ocean, and all the universes are but its waves. A special music comes forth from it, the primordial sound that creates the worlds. It contains the highest stage of speech, the supreme silence which is the revelation I-am-that-I-am. It is the origin and support of all mantras, where all mantras become one and universal. There we contact the voice of the original teacher or guru, who is the source of all genuine guidance and all true scriptures, the very word of God. There we discover our true ancestry and lineage, the sages and seers who have helped humanity from time immemorial. There we contact the supreme Beloved, the Divine Father and Mother, whom we all seek for grace. The heart space is the heaven of all true devotion, beyond all form, division and limitation, where all the Gods and Goddesses become one.

> **The space within the heart is our true home.**

Those who do not know the space within the heart have missed the most important thing in life. They have condemned themselves to be ever seeking and striving and never come to rest. Because we are afraid of being nothing, we must ever struggle to become something. We fall from spirit, which is immaterial, into matter, which being formed is mortal, limited and uncertain. We lose our inner space and become an outer thing, a mere body or person confined within a few feet of flesh. We give up our light and become a shadow of what other people think.

True meditation is returning to the space within the heart. It consists of withdrawing and immersing the mind in the inner heart space, in which the mind gets lost and loses itself like a drop within the sea. This requires that we sink deep inside ourselves, merging everything within the core of our being.

Yet while easy to understand conceptually and not difficult to feel emotionally, a complete merging into the inner space is not easy. Though the most direct it is also the most difficult of all practices and the fruit of all. Few advanced yogis are able to accomplish it, even after years of practice. To move into the spiritual heart requires that we withdraw our entire attention from the field of the senses, directing all of our energy within. A tremendous fire of spiritual practice is necessary to get there. It requires an inward death and transfiguration even while the body is alive. To really fully return to the spiritual heart requires the consummate energization of our entire life and consciousness. Yet any contact with the spiritual heart, however minor, must sow the seeds of its eventual realization.

To open that space within we must release the knots of fear and desire that bind us to the outer world. We must let go of all the stress and tension that we create around ourselves trying to sustain a personal life or promote a personal identity. Space is our true nature. We must open our hearts to the inner space of pure awareness. That is the ultimate goal of all life, the beginning and end of everything, of which all that we know is but a shadow.

The True Self

T he Self is the Self. Its identity is intrinsic: "I am who I am," "I am that I am." The Self has no identity. It is pure identity, Being itself. In the Self we are all that we see, and to see is to be. This is the ultimate equation, the solution to all questions, in which all things become One.

The true Self can never be another. It can never be a thing. To think that "I am this" or "I am that" is to lose identity as the pure "I am." To think "I need this" or "I need that" is to become caught in a stream of dependency because the external can never be intrinsic or independent. To have an image of one's Self is to lose the Self, to make it into a commodity. To become something is to lose one's identity as the pure Subject and become an object among objects in an uncertain world.

We suffer because we do not have a Self. Our identity is dependent upon some thing or person that we are connected with. Identity that is dependent, that is given by another—like a name or title—is a fiction. It is a superimposition of thought, and though it may distract us for a time, it cannot afford us peace.

We suffer because we seek the Self in the notself, the Subject in the object. We try to find happiness by achievement and acquisition in the external world. But achievement is becoming a bigger or better object. Acquisition is the accumulation of objects around our assumed objectivity or materiality. But to be an object is to be heavy, dependent and transient. Objectivity is not a state of happiness or fulfillment. Happiness is only possible in eternal existence, which is only possible in the pure Subject. As long as we think we need something to be ourselves, we will always be dependent on another. We will always be somebody else or trying to please someone else. We will never be ourselves but will be trapped in the conditioned responses around us. We will be victims of other people's thoughts.

The true Self is not the ego. It is not the "I am this" or the "I want that." It is devoid of any self-image. Even to call it a self can be misleading because it belongs to no one and nothing belongs to it. Yet it is who we naturally are. It is the state of pure seeing devoid of any objectification of self or other.

There is no need but that we be the Self—that we not be another and not become somebody for others. We need only be as we are. Moreover, we should not turn other subjects, which are but different manifestations of our Self, into objects. All is the Self or intrinsic being. In that all beings are redeemed, all life is delivered, and existence itself is fulfillment.

The Subject can never be an object. The Self cannot be the body, the senses, the mind or emotions. It cannot have any role, status or appearance in the outer world or in the world of thought. A subject that is also an object is a misconception that breeds illusion and suffering. It is a false logic, the logic of the ignorance that equates consciousness with an object, form or quality. It is the cosmic blunder, the great error of the soul, the fall that creates all confusion and misery.

Whatever has form, quality, name, image or action is an object. Whatever has consciousness is in essence the pure Subject and not affected by the objects in its field of perception. Just as a cup falling from a table and breaking does not hurt us though we observe it, so the qualities of our body and mind do not affect or hurt the true Self, though we observe them intimately.

We must question this objectification of ourselves and of others. There is no identity in anything because all objects are transient, dependent and composite. They have nothing intrinsic. Identity is only possible in Being itself. There is only one pure or absolute identity, which is to be all. Any relative or limited identity is a fiction of this confusion between subject and object. Only when we have divested ourselves of all objectivity can we know the truth of who we really are.

Visualization

$\left(\mathbf{V}\right)$ isualization is a helpful tool to calm the mind. A harmonious visualization helps settle the weight of negative impressions reverberating in the subconscious while creating a harmonious impression that gives peace. For such visualizations various objects can be used, as long as the intention is spiritual. One may visualize the form of a God or a Goddess, or a great teacher. One may imagine some aspect of nature like the sky, the ocean, a mountain, river or forest. One may look at a flame, a leaf or a flower. One may take a more abstract approach and visualize a color, a geometrical form or yantra. Each has its specific value.

Yet such visualization is preliminary to the real practice of meditation. Once the mind has been brought into a harmonious state, one should proceed with a deeper meditation to discover the true Self. Visualization serves to calm the outer mind and senses and direct us within, which is its real utility. It is like setting the stage for the main event.

However, visualization should not be used for trying to get what we want or achieving our ego aims, which will only trap us further in the realm of desire. While visualization done properly can help us move beyond our conditioning, done improperly it can reinforce our conditioning and increase the weight of negative impressions. We must be honest with ourselves about what we are seeking through visualization, or it will not serve our spiritual quest.

The Way of the Actual
and the Way of the Ideal

T here are two primary ways to alter the contents of our consciousness. The first is to observe them for what they actually are, to witness the mind and its movements, like watching a river flow. In this process we transcend the limitations of the mind into the witnessing awareness beyond thought. We observe our shifting contradictory fears and desires, and discard them by the power of seeing.

The second way is to cultivate the ideal, which is to ignore the actual and its limitations and look to a greater reality beyond our personal becoming. This is to affirm the One, Infinite, Eternal Being, the Divine Self within all beings. In this process we lose interest in the contents of consciousness and contact the light of awareness behind the ideal that we seek. While the way of observation is mainly part of the yoga of knowledge, the cultivation of the ideal is primarily a way of devotion.

Yet to properly cultivate the ideal requires a sincere and constant aspiration. It cannot be arrived at through mere desire or imagination. It requires a genuine opening at a heart level. The ideal must be a living flame, not a mere hope or expectation.

The way of the actual is essentially a negative approach. It does not posit anything positive but discards the negative by seeing it for what it is. The way of the ideal is a positive approach. It gives up concern with the negative by immersing the mind in the higher states. Both methods have their usage and their limitations. If we get too involved with the actual we can lose our higher aspiration and get trapped in the movements of the mind, which are endless. We become that which we give our attention to. If we give our attention to the neurotic mind we become the neurotic mind. On the other hand, if we superficially pursue the ideal we get lost in fantasy and wishful thinking and fail to deal with our real problems. For clarity we must see the actual as it is but also be open to the reality of the ideal beyond.

Yoga and Meditation

$\left(\begin{array}{c}Y\end{array}\right)$ oga in the classical sense is the process through which the mind is silenced and transcended. It is not merely a set of physical postures or breathing practices. Its chief method is meditation, not any outer action, though these have their place in its unfoldment.

Yogic postures bring calm and balance to the body. Yogic breathing brings harmony and energy to the vital force. While these are of great value, they cannot in themselves take us beyond thought. They must be used as the foundation for meditation, or their application is incomplete. Mental techniques like mantra and visualization are additional important aids for meditation. They stabilize the thought process, which is necessary to allow it to be put to rest. However, if we do not look beyond them to the Divine consciousness within ourselves, they can eventually become obstacles.

While many tools and practices have been invented to facilitate the practice of yoga, the main process of yoga is very simple. It is to no longer look outward to find truth or happiness, but to rest in our real nature, what yoga calls the *Purusha* or higher Self, free of all other considerations. This inner abidance requires inquiry and surrender, which are the two main aspects of all yoga practices. Inquiry means tracing our thought process back to its origin in consciousness. Surrender means faith in the inner reality and relinquishing our outer seeking in order to enter into it.

> Yogic postures bring calm and balance to the body.

Without some sort of practice of yoga, which means meditation, we cannot get beyond our human problems. All other practices, however useful, will not prove sufficient to bring about a real change in ourselves or in our society. Therefore, we must once more return to the science and practice of yoga as the basis of our culture. This is not a mere matter of doing yoga postures in the morning but requires that our entire life be rooted in consciousness and meditation.

Meditation requires that we give space to what is beyond name and form to reveal itself—that we set aside our opinions and come to commune with things as they are. This is only possible when we give up our belief in matter or the known and give our prime value to awareness itself. Through meditation we enter into a new dimension of existence where fulfillment lies in seeing. We no longer require either sensation or thought to make us feel alive. This state of seeing allows us to merge into the entire universe and beyond. This is the real goal of yoga.

PART IV

The Teachings of Ramana Maharshi

The unchanging reality dwells within the heart. It shines by itself, how can anyone write about it?

In the middle of the lotus of the heart, supreme as the Absolute, the pure I is directly perceived. It shines by the nature of the Self.

Enter into the heart, diving with your mind and your thoughts or by control of the breath. Be one who abides in the Self.

> Ramana Maharshi,
> *Three Verses on Liberation (Muktatrayam)*

Ramana Maharshi is probably the foremost modern teacher of Vedanta, specifically the path of Self-inquiry. In this section of the book we will examine his teaching in his own words. This material is a bit more technical and reflects a traditional style of expression.

Upadesha Saram:
The Essence of Instruction of
Sri Ramana Maharshi

(U) *padesha Saram* means "the essence of instruction." It suc-
cinctly explains the Vedantic view of yoga and meditation
from the perspective of a realized soul. In this teaching the illus-
trious sage Bhagavan Ramana Maharshi explains all the main
yogic practices culminating in the practice of Self-inquiry. IIe
shows how aspirants grow and mature from preliminary ritualis-
tic practices into the higher knowledge and finally into Self-realization. The first half of the teaching deals with foundational
practices of service, devotion, mantra and pranayama. The
second half explains the yoga of knowledge (Jnana Yoga) and
its various methods. That so much could be contained in a few
verses is quite amazing, to say the least. I have used my own
translation and added a commentary to bring out the implications
of this condensed teaching. Ramana Maharshi's words are in bold
type; my commentary is in regular roman type.

Recognizing the Law of Karma

1. By the command of the Creator one gains the fruits of
   one's deeds. Karma is not supreme. Karma by itself is
   inert.

2. Karma makes us fall into the vast ocean of repeated
   action. Its fruit is transient and it prevents us from
   achieving our goal of liberation.

To start on the spiritual path we must first recognize the law of
karma. We must understand that we create our own destiny
through our actions in this and previous lives. Through karma

we fall into the cycle of rebirth and its resultant sorrows of birth and death, which is the real cause of our unhappiness in life.

But karma is not supreme and does not exist by itself. Karma accrues owing to the will of God, who rules this universe by impartial law. Recognizing that karma depends upon the Divine will, we cease to pursue the fruits of action and look to the real power behind the universe to guide us.

Karma binds us to the world of impermanence and prevents us from contacting the freedom of our eternal nature. Recognizing this, we gain detachment from outer actions, which is the necessary basis of all yogic practices.

The Need for Karma Yoga

> 3. Action dedicated to the Lord, not done by desire, is the means of purifying the mind and of facilitating liberation.

Karma Yoga is the beginning of spiritual practice. The way out of the web of karma is through Karma Yoga or selfless service— action dedicated to God. Selfless action purifies our minds and bodies and puts our lives in harmony with the Divine will. It is not karma itself that binds us but desire for its results. Desireless action is the foundation of the spiritual path and all of its methods, which should be free from selfish motivation.

Ritual, Mantra and Meditation: The Three Foundational Practices

> 4. The supreme duties of body, speech and mind are ritual, mantra and meditation.

On the basis of Karma Yoga we must reorient all our faculties. Our nature compels us to act. Liberating action consists of spiritual practices. These are threefold according to the three aspects of our nature as body, speech and mind. Our supreme bodily duty is ritual action, which is twofold as worship of god and as service to humanity. The supreme duty of speech is mantra or repetition of Divine names. The supreme duty of the mind is meditation.

The Twofold Karma Yoga

5. Service to the world should be done with the thought of God. One should ritually worship the Lord, who takes the form of the eight aspects of creation.

Karma Yoga is twofold as selfless service *(seva)* for the benefit of all living beings and as devotional worship *(puja)* to the Divine in various forms. Service to the world should take place with the thought that the world is a manifestation of God. True ritual worship, as of Divine images, should be based upon the recognition of the Divine presence in the world, the Creator who takes the form of the eight aspects of creation. These are the five elements, the mind, ego and nature; all are embodied in the different aspects of traditional pujas. Without an inner recognition of the Divine, any practice of service or ritual remains mechanical and ineffective. Note that yogic asanas come under ritual as a form of bodily practice and should be done as a form of worship.

Mantra Yoga

6. Better than loud chanting of mantras is their soft muttering. Best is their mental repetition.

Mantra yoga deals with speech, and is the next stage after Karma Yoga, which deals with the body. Repetition of mantras takes three forms. Loud chanting helps us imbibe the basic quality of the mantra and purifies the vocal organ. Soft muttering of mantras connects them with the breath, which it energizes as a force of awareness. Mental repetition, in which mantras reverberate in the subconscious, has the strongest transformative effect and can change the nature of the mind. Practicing mantras in these three stages and holding them at the third stage is the best.

The Ramanashram, Ramana's ashram, since Ramana's time holds daily Vedic chanting for its power to calm and purify the mind. Ramana also recommended the chanting of mantras like OM and various Divine names, particularly the name of Shiva or Arunachala mountain *(OM Arunachala Shivaya Namah!)*. When the mind is harmonized through mantra, a peaceful meditation can easily proceed and endure.

Concentration

> 7. Like the flow of oil in a steady stream, a simple and sustained stream of thought is better than that which is complex and broken.

Meditation, of whatever type, should be based upon concentration *(dharana)*. It should follow a simple, pure and unbroken current like a pouring stream of warm *ghee* (clarified butter).

Bhakti Yoga

> 8. From meditation on difference, one proceeds to meditating on "He am I." Meditation without a sense of difference is regarded as the most purifying.

Once concentration develops, one begins with meditation on forms, such as those of deities like Shiva, Vishnu or the Goddess. This is the basis of Bhakti Yoga, the yoga of devotion. At first one sees these deities as different from oneself. Then by degree one comes to understand that the Gods are merely forms of one's own deeper Self, the Divine presence in the heart. This culminates in the realization, "He (the Self within the Deity) am I." One comes to meditate upon the deity as oneself. This seeing of the Self in the deity is the real purifying power, not the particular form that one uses, however useful that is as a vehicle.

Ramana himself worshipped Lord Shiva, experiencing directly the "form path" of Bhakti Yoga. He also worshipped the Goddess. Many of Ramana's great devotees worshipped Ramana himself in the form of Lord Skanda, the son of Shiva, or as Dakshinamurti, the youthful form of Shiva.

Formless Devotion

9. From the absence of any particular mental state comes abidance in the state of being. From the strength of that feeling comes the highest devotion.

Devotion on its higher levels becomes formless. Once one goes beyond the feeling for a particular deity and its name and form, one comes to the state of pure being. From the strength of feeling that pure being in all life comes the highest devotion, which is to see the Self in all beings and all beings in the Self.

Abidance in the Heart, the Essence of All the Yogas

10. When the mind attains composure in its abode within the heart, this is the essence of Karma, Bhakti, Yoga and Jnana.

The essence of all yogic practices is returning to the origin of the mind within the heart. Though the different yogas have their different methods, their goal is the same. Note that the Maharshi first explains Karma, Mantra and Bhakti Yogas as the basis for Jnana Yoga, the yoga of knowledge. In the following verses Ramana focuses on how to abide in the heart, using two main methods of Yoga (meaning here control of prana) and Jnana (mind control), as the heart is the source of both mind and prana.

Pranayama

11. By controlling the breath, the mind comes to rest like a bird in a net. Breath control is a means to control the mind.

By controlling the prana one can control the mind. This is the basis of yogic teachings that emphasize pranayama. Only rare advanced aspirants can control the mind directly. For most practitioners pranayama is a great aid to control the mind. Through deepening the breath one draws one's attention within, and the mind loses its pull to the external world. This is likened to catching a restless bird in a net.

Ramana taught that if one is not in the company of a great yogi, pranayama is the best method to gain power for one's practice. Those of us who don't have such exalted company or circumstances to inspire us should not forget pranayama. Pranayama purifies the body and energizes the mind for meditation. It helps us control the unruly senses that draw the mind outward.

Unity of Mind and Prana

12. Mind and prana are endowed with knowledge and action. They are two branches whose root is a common power.

The mind is the power of knowledge and prana is the power of action. They are like the two wings of a bird. Knowledge implies action and action requires knowledge. Both mind and prana have a common power behind them, which is that of the Self. One can control both by going to their root energy, the power of consciousness.

Mind Control

13. Mergence and dissolution are the two types of mind control. The mind that is merged will rise up again. The dissolved mind is dead.

14. Through control of the prana, the mind is merged. From meditation on the One, the mind is dissolved.

15. The superior yogi has a dissolved mind. What further duty can he have, who abides in his own nature?

Breath control temporarily suspends the mind. Self-knowledge dissolves the mind permanently. Therefore, however useful a tool breath control can be, without advancing to mind control the aim of dissolving the mind cannot be attained. So one should use pranayama as a means to mind control and not stop short with it as the goal. The highest yogi goes beyond prana and mind by the power of meditation.

Pratyahara: Control of the Senses

16. The mind dissolved in the Self repels all objectivity. The vision of pure consciousness is the vision of truth.

The key to dissolving the mind is turning one's attention away from external objects. This is the practice of *pratyahara* or control of the outgoing mind and senses. This control of the senses is the link between control of prana and control of the mind. The senses mediate between the mind (our thoughts and feelings) and prana (our vital urges).

Ramana himself practiced total pratyahara, simulating the death experience and drawing all his prana into the heart when he had his Self-realization as a lad of sixteen. Without withdrawal from sensory activity and external attachments, the practice of Self-inquiry is like gathering water in a vessel with holes in it. Therefore, pratyahara should be practiced first as the basis for meditation. Having explained mind control in general, Ramana now focuses on the specific methods of Self-inquiry that bring it about.

The Direct Path

17. What is the nature of the mind? When one looks for the mind, it disappears. This is the direct path.

When pratyahara has been achieved and one has turned completely away from the world, one can look directly into the nature of the mind. However, without the support of an external object to depend on, the mind, which is a form of external conditioning, itself disappears. This is the direct path. If we look for the mind we will not find it because the mind itself is a form of external seeking that is removed by the introversion of awareness. In the very seeking of the mind, the mind disappears.

Self-Inquiry

18. All mental activities are rooted in the I-thought. The mind is its thoughts. Know that the ego is the mind.

19. Meditating "from where does this I come" the ego falls away. This is Self-inquiry.

20. When the ego is destroyed, the pure I as the heart opens by itself as the supreme fullness of being.

The practice of Self-inquiry involves tracing the I-thought back to its origin in the spiritual heart. Returning the mind and ego to the heart, one discovers infinite being as one's true awareness. This is Ramana's most characteristic teaching and the main path of the yoga of knowledge.

Deep Sleep

21. This heart is known by the word "I" in our daily experience. Even when the ego is forgotten in deep sleep, it continues as our foundational being.

Another method of Self-inquiry is to trace our waking consciousness back to the awareness that persists even in deep sleep when the mind is put to rest. That deep-sleep I is the real Self, while the waking ego is an illusion. Once one has learned Self-inquiry in the waking state, one must carry it over to dream and deep sleep for it to become really efficacious. At the origin of all our mental activities is the Divine I am, but we must return to that origin behind the veil of sleep and ignorance in order to realize it.

Discrimination Between the Seer and the Seen

22. I am not the body, the senses, the prana, the intellect or the ignorance behind them. I am the Unitary Being. That which is dependent is non-being.

Yet another method is to discriminate between the seer and the seen. This is done on all levels of our being. We must learn to differentiate our true Self, subjectivity and sentience from our various bodies, vehicles or instruments that depend upon it. This practice starts with the physical body, which is an instrument of action. Then we move to the senses, which are instruments of knowledge. Then we proceed to prana, which is the power of action, and ultimately to the mind, representing the power of knowing. The Self that these depend upon is different and abides in the heart behind all these instruments and their fluctuations.

We must practice Self-inquiry not only on a conceptual level but in our physical, sensory and pranic activities as well. Self-inquiry is not just tracing the movement of thought into the heart but placing our entire existence there.

Pure Consciousness

23. As the illuminator of Being, how can Consciousness be different from it? Consciousness exists as Being. That consciousness exists as I.

Another method is to see being as consciousness and consciousness as the pure I or pure subjectivity. I-am-that-I-am is I-am-all or Being is all. Once we have returned to that Unitary Being we realize it as pure consciousness and the true Self.

Merging God and the Soul in the Supreme Self

24. God and the soul are distinguished by their vestures. Their Self-nature as pure being is the supreme reality.

25. By eliminating the vestures in the perception of the Self-nature, the vision of God takes the form of the Self.

God and the soul are the two ultimate factors behind the universe, which is their field of action. These two differ only by their vestures. God has an all-powerful mind and prana. The soul has a limited mind and prana. Yet their common Self-nature unites them in the supreme reality. The way to unite God and the individual soul is to negate their vestures and recognize the common Consciousness behind them. One can only truly know

God as the Self. Otherwise knowledge of God is indirect and not real.

Abidance in the Self

26. The state of the Self is the perception of the Self. From the non-dual nature of the Self arises abidance in the Self.

To see is to be. To see the Self is to be the Self. To be the Self is to see the Self. Meditating on the unity of being and seeing is another important approach. Actually there is no approach because the Self simply is what it is.

Beyond the Known

27. Consciousness devoid of knowing and not knowing is the real knowledge. What else is there to know?

Another method is to meditate on "What is knowledge?" The highest knowledge is devoid of any object to be known. It is self-luminous, self-aware wisdom. The highest knowing is going beyond knowledge. This is not a mere theoretical leap but a revolution at the core of consciousness.

Bliss Absolute

28. What is the Self-nature? In the perception of the Self is the immutable, unborn, consciousness bliss absolute.

29. He who here attains the supreme bliss beyond bondage and release is a Divine soul.

Another method is to search out the source of bliss or true happiness. That lies in the Self, not in any external object. It is found only in consciousness, not in any material achievement.

The soul becomes Divine by achieving that state beyond bondage and release. This is the supreme goal of practice that is beyond all goals. To reach it is a Divine gift that follows from the practices set forth in the previous verses. This bliss is the origin and end of everything.

Ramana's Teaching

30. One's own awareness free of the ego—this is the great austerity and the Word of Ramana.

This pure awareness beyond the separate self is the highest knowledge. But it is not conceptual. It is like a great fire. It is the *tapas* or ascetic practice that Ramana proved in his daily actions. Ramana did not simply talk about Self-realization or teach it as a mere theory, fantasy or emotion. He lived it, to the extent that he had no real body consciousness at all. This teaching is also Ramana's Divine Word. It arose from the Divine Word in the heart and is not a product of human thought or ego, even Ramana's.

It is easy to read such teachings and not difficult to understand them logically. One can use them to create a mental or emotional high. But their true realization is another matter and requires much practice. To reach that we must dedicate ourselves to the task in all that we do and are.

The Teachings of
Ramana Maharshi:
An Integral View

As a follow-up to *Upadesha Saram* I have added a further explanation of the different methods that Bhagavan Ramana Maharshi taught. Though Ramana emphasized Self-inquiry, a careful examination of his teachings reveals that he recommended various yogic approaches of devotion, mantra and pranayama—in fact, he encouraged whatever might aid a person in his or her practice. All such practices he reinterpreted as aids to or methods of Self-inquiry.

The Maharshi did not put much emphasis on outer formalities of Self-inquiry, such as the rules of monasticism, but he did recognize the importance of various prerequisites and aids to the practice. He particularly emphasized a pure vegetarian diet as a crucial aid for clarity of mind. He noted the importance of *satsanga* or communion with spiritual teachers and aspirants. Pilgrimage to holy sites like Arunachala mountain was significant to him as well. Daily Vedic chanting occurs at his ashram to create an environment suitable for meditation. The Maharshi's path follows the integral approach of Vedic teachings going back thousands of years and, particularly, the Advaitic and yogic approaches taught by the great sage Shankaracharya (seventh century) that include devotional and yoga practices.

Actually all yogic practices should be forms of *vichara* or inquiry into our true nature. Whether it is asana, pranayama, mantra or meditation, all are prescribed to gain knowledge of the Atman or Purusha, which is the goal of yoga as stated in the *Yoga Sutras* (I.3) as "abidance in the Self-nature of the Seer." Whatever yogic practices one does should be performed out of an attitude of inner inquiry or observation. In this way they all contribute to Self-inquiry and broaden its practice to encompass all aspects of our life.

Common Root of Thought, Breath and Speech

We have already discussed how all thoughts are rooted in the I-thought that arises from the pure consciousness in the heart. But the heart is the origin of prana and speech as well. In fact it is the origin of everything. Mind, prana and speech have a common source in the heart that is the fountain of awareness, energy and creativity.

Just as our thoughts arise from the I-thought in the heart, so our breath arises from the great Prana in the heart. So too, our speech arises from the Divine Word or unstruck sound *(anahata shabda)* in the heart, the OM current. Self-inquiry can work by tracing the origins of prana and speech into the heart, just as following our thoughts can do it.

Inquiry into the Word or Speech: Mantra-Vichara

This practice involves tracing the origin of sound and speech in the heart. For it one can use any mantra, particularly seed syllables (bija mantras) like OM or HREEM, which exist at the level of primal sound. One repeats the sound first orally and then mentally, taking the sound current back to the inner silence at the core of our being.

Prana Vichara—Pranayama as Self-inquiry

This involves tracing the origin of the breath and the vital force into the heart. One can practice a simple, effortless pranayama like *So-ham* pranayama, meditating upon the mantra "So" on inhalation and "Ham" on exhalation, letting the breath naturally deepen. One should take one's attention along with the breath down to the heart on inhalation and up from the heart on exhalation, abiding in the heart on retention.

Another way is to practice pranayama while holding to the witnessing Self as the source of prana in the heart. One observes the ebb and flow of the breath from the space of awareness in the heart. It is not enough to inquire into our Self merely with the outer mind; we should do so with our full vitality or prana.

Tracing the Senses to the Heart

The senses originate from the light of consciousness in the heart. The light of consciousness from the heart reflects up and outward through the head, diversifying through the senses like a lamp shining through different windows. From the current of the mind from the heart to the head the seven currents of the sensory openings in the head emerge (two eyes, two ears, two nostrils and mouth).

Another method is to witness the senses. The Self, as the *Upanishads* say, is the eye of the eye and the ear of the ear. One can witness the sense of sound by holding to a state of pure listening or the inner ear. One can witness the sense of sight by holding to the consciousness of the seer or the inner eye.

Self-inquiry should be practiced with all the senses. Only if we have control of the senses can we control our attention and the mind itself.

Withdrawal into the Heart: Pratyahara

When Ramana Maharshi gained his Self-realization as a mere lad of sixteen he first simulated the death experience and then inquired: "Who am I?". This simulated death experience is Pratyahara, in which one withdraws the mind, prana and senses into the heart. Such a withdrawal is necessary for Self-inquiry to be complete. As long as our energy and attention flow outward we cannot merge them back into the inner Self. For this the aspirant should consciously withdraw his or her attention from various limbs of the body back into the heart.

Another method of Pratyahara is practicing silence or not speaking *(mauna)*. This internalizes the power of attention. All who practice Self-inquiry should learn the Pratyahara of the heart, placing all attention and energy into the heart as the foundation for meditation. This is to die to external involvements on a daily basis.

Bhakti Yoga

Bhakti Yoga, the path of devotion, consists of surrender to the Divine within the heart. The Maharshi considered it the most important yoga path after Self-inquiry and usually recommended the two together. Surrender can be done in four ways:

1. Surrender to the Supreme Self *(Atma-Bhakti)*
2. Surrender to God or the Cosmic Lord as a formless being *(Ishvara-Bhakti)*
3. Surrender to God in the form of various Gods or Goddesses *(Ishta-Devata-Bhakti)*
4. Surrender to God in the form of the Guru *(Guru-Bhakti)*

Formless devotional approaches, like surrender to the light of truth, are not necessarily better because devotion generally depends upon a form. As our basic attachment is to form, to direct our feeling to a Divine form can make us attached to God as the source of our being. Such a personally chosen deity is called an *Ishta-Devata*.

Hinduism provides many Gods and Goddesses like Shiva, Vishnu and the Goddess, which represent different names and forms of Divinity, to appeal to the different temperaments of individuals. Different avatars or great teachers, like Rama, Krishna or Buddha, can be used as well. One can choose whatever devotional form most appeals to one's heart. Usually the name or mantra of the deity is repeated, along with meditation upon their form or presence as residing in the heart, and as representing one's true Self.

Karma Yoga

We all must act or work in life. Karma Yoga is the way to use our actions for spiritual growth. It has two forms for its deeper practice:

1. Holding to the attitude of the non-doer or witnessing Self in the midst of all actions.
2. Surrendering to God as the real doer in the midst of all actions.

The first Karma Yoga approach is allied with the yoga of knowledge as a form of inquiry, the second to the yoga of devotion as a form of surrender. Selfless service is not out of harmony with Self-realization. Today, at this time of global crisis, many Vedantins are taking up social action, not as a substitute for their inner practices but as an expression of them. Self-knowledge is the real basis for social action that can raise up the world according to its Divine ideal.

Through employing an integral practice of yoga in its different forms from the perspective of Self-inquiry, the aspirant will gain a better foundation for practice and achieve more lasting results.

May all those who attempt the practice gain success!

May all those who begin it persevere whatever the obstacles!

Glossary

Agni – The flame of awareness
Advaita – Non-duality
Ahamkara – Ego
Ananda – Bliss
Asana – Yoga posture
Atman – Higher Self
Atma-Vichara – Self-inquiry
Bhakti – Devotion
Brahman – Absolute, God or Godhead
Buddhi – Higher Mind, Intelligence
Chit – Consciousness
Dharana – Concentration
Dharma – Natural law, cosmic law, truth principle
Dhyana – Meditation
Ishta-Devata – Personal Deity chosen for devotional purposes
Ishvara – Creator, God
Jnana – Knowledge (spiritual or Self-knowledge)
Karma – Action
Kundalini – Power of Consciousness residing in the human
   being
Manas – Mind
Mantra – Sacred words or sounds like OM
Maya – Illusion
Nirvana – The Divine realm or realm of enlightenment and
   peace
Prana – Vital force or breath
Pranayama – Control of the breath
Pratyahara – Control of the senses
Puja – Ritual

Purusha – Higher Self, Atman

Samadhi – Spiritual realization

Samsara – The world of illusion

Sat – Being

Satsanga – Communion among spiritual aspirants

Sattva – Quality of purity

Shakti – Power of consciousness

Upanishads – Key Vedantic scriptures or source books

Vedas – Core mantric teachings behind Vedanta; ancient scriptures of India

Vedanta – Vedic path of Self-realization

Vichara – Meditative inquiry

Yoga – Practices aiming at union with the Divine

Bibliography

Aurobindo, Sri. *The Upanishads*. Twin Lakes, Wisconsin: Lotus Press, 1999.

Baba, Bangali. *The Yoga Sutras of Patanjali*. Delhi, India: Motilal Banarsidass, 1982.

Dayananda, Swami. *Introduction to Vedanta*. New Delhi, India: Vision Books, 1993.

Dayananda, Swami. *Talks On Upsadesa Saram of Ramana Maharshi*. Rishikesh, India: Sri Gangadhareswar Trust, 1987.

Dayton, Brandt, Editor. *The Practical Vedanta of Swami Rama Tirtha*. Honesdale, Pennsylvania: Himalayan Institute, 1978.

Feuerstein, Kak, and Frawley. *In Search of the Cradle of Civilization*. Wheaton, Illinois: Quest Books, 1995.

Frawley, David. *Ayurveda and the Mind: The Healing of Consciousness*. Twin Lakes, Wisconsin: Lotus Press, 1997.

Frawley, David. *Yoga and Ayurveda: Self-Healing and Self-Realization*. Twin Lakes, Wisconsin: Lotus Press, 1999.

Maharshi, Ramana. *Ramana Gita*. Tiruvannamalai, India: Sri Ramanasramam, 1998.

Maharshi, Ramana. *Talks with Ramana Maharshi*. Tiruvannamalai, India: Sri Ramanasramam, 1978.

Maharshi, Ramana. *Upadesasara*. Tiruvannamalai, India: Sri Ramanasramam, 1987.

Shivananda, Swami. *Shivananda Upanishad* (Compiled by Swami Vishnudevananda). Val Morin, Canada: Shivananda Ashram, 1995.

Vivekananda, Swami. *The Complete Works of Swami Vivekananda*. Calcutta, India: Advaita Ashram, 1992.

Yogananda, Paramahansa. *God Talks with Arjuna: The Bhagavad Gita*. Los Angeles, California: Self-Realization Fellowship, 1995.

About the Author

(D) avid Frawley has been a student of Ramana Maharshi's teachings since 1970 and has written for their magazine *The Mountain Path* since 1978. He is a visiting professor at the Sringeri Shankaracharya Math, the oldest Vedantic center in India, and has received the personal blessings of the Shankaracharya. He teaches at Vedantic centers in America and is one of the few Westerners recognized as an authentic Vedantic teacher by the Vishva Hindu Parishad, the largest Hindu religious organization in the world.

He directs the American Institute of Vedic Studies in Santa Fe, New Mexico. He can be reached at:

American Institute of Vedic Studies
P.O. Box 8357
Santa Fe NM 87504-8357
David Frawley (Vamadeva Shastri), Director
Phone: 505-983-9385, Fax: 505-982-5807
Web: www.vedanet.com, Email: vedicinst@aol.com